THE CITIES OF
ROMAN AFRICA

THE CITIES OF
ROMAN
AFRICA

GARETH SEARS

The
History
Press

First published 2011

The History Press
The Mill, Brimscombe Port
Stroud, Gloucestershire, GL5 2QG
www.thehistorypress.co.uk

British Library Cataloguing in Publication Data.
A catalogue record for this book is available from the British Library.

ISBN 978 0 7524 4843 5

Typesetting and origination by The History Press
Printed in Great Britain
Manufacturing managed by Jellyfish Print Solutions Ltd

Contents

Note on Illustrations

All photographs were taken by the author with the exception of Colour Plates 2 and 10, which were taken by Mr Ed Cooley; Figures 5.1, 6.2, 6.3 and 6.6, which were taken by Mr Graham Norrie; and Figure 4.1 and Colour Plate 21, which were taken by Dr Roger White. The copyright for all of these photographs remains with the photographer. All plans and maps were redrawn and edited by Mr Henry Buglass using the sources listed below. My thanks go to all of my colleagues and Ed for their help with the images. The bibliography contains full references for all of the books used unless otherwise stated.

Abbreviations

Much of the evidence for urban life in Roman Africa comes from Latin inscriptions. The following abbreviations for inscription corpora will be used:

AE – *L'Année Epigraphique*
CIL – *Corpus Inscriptionum Latinarum*
ILAfr. – *Inscriptions Latines de l'Afrique*
ILAlg. – *Inscriptions latines de l'Algérie*
ILS – *Inscriptiones Latinae Selectae*
ILTun. – *Inscriptions latines de la Tunisie*
IRT – *Inscriptions of Roman Tripolitania*

Latin inscriptions from the Roman Empire are brought together on the searchable *Clauss-Slaby Epigraphik Datenbank* – www.manfredclauss.de/gb/index.html

I have used a few abbreviations for literary sources. They are:

Amm. – Ammianus Marcellinus
Appian – *Libyca* – Roman History: Libyan War
August. – Augustine of Hippo
Conf. – *Confessions*
Cons. ev. – *On the Consensus of the Evangelists*
De civ. Dei – *On the City of God*
En. in Ps. – *Expositions on the Psalms*
Ep. – *Letters*

Serm. – *Sermons*
Haer. – *On Heresies*
Optatus – Optatus of Milevis, *Against the Donatists*
Pliny, *H.N.* – Natural History
Sallust, *B.Jug.* – *Jugurthan War*
Salvian, *Gub. Dei.* – *On the Governance of God*
SHA – *The Augustan History*
CTh – *Theodosian Code*

Introduction

The inhabitants of Roman Africa produced flourishing, continuously evolving urban cultures. They produced one of the Empire's largest cities in Carthage, the stunningly wealthy Lepcis Magna, Thysdrus (El Djem) and its vast amphitheatre and a large number of small monumentalised towns, such as Thugga. This book will examine why the inhabitants of Africa produced this culture, these cities. It was created through their choices and actions (Giddens 1984), through their reactions to the realities of imperial power and by the access that the Roman Empire gave them to new ideas, fashions and technologies. These cities did not just appear in the form preserved in the archaeological record. They were not an inevitable consequence of African and Roman communication, but were created through the decisions of their people, specifically the elites, as they responded to the interaction of cultures within a particular geographic region within a series of ecological and climatic zones. Just as their inhabitants created the cities, so the cities moulded their populations. The buildings and the activities that went on in them helped to condition Africans to become proper Romans. They helped to inculcate beliefs across generations and were the environment in which the rhythms of urban life could be played out. The city was also the basic unit of administration. It was in the cities that much taxation was collected and passed on to the centre or the army; it was in the city that most crime was punished and it was in the city that most religious rituals to keep the gods happy occurred. The city was crucial to the proper functioning of the Roman Empire.

The Cities of Roman Africa will examine the creation and evolution of these cities and the urban culture they housed throughout the whole period of the Roman Empire. It will consider the structures, primarily the public buildings and open spaces that were created, and the activities that went on in and around them. What this book cannot be is a comprehensive study of every city in every period; individual cities were products of their own individual histories as well as a wider cultural history.

Instead we will examine the major developments through a wide range of case studies within the broad definition of 'city' and in doing so will consider what it meant to be 'urban' in Roman Africa.

In terms of geographical spread urban communities in modern western Libya, Tunisia, Algeria and Morocco – the Latin speaking parts of Roman Africa – shall be examined. The cities of eastern Libya (ancient Cyrenaica) or Egypt, which were very different in terms of their origins and development and where the culturally dominant language was Greek, will not be covered. In the Roman period our region was divided into a series of provinces which for the majority of the period were, from east to west, Africa Proconsularis (later divided into Proconsularis, Byzacena and Tripolitania), Numidia (after the early third century), Mauretania Caesarensis and Mauretania Tingitana (see Maps 2–5). Tingitana was somewhat divorced from the other provinces because of the distances involved and the effect of the Atlas Mountains on communications. In consequence relatively little attention will be paid to the few Roman cities in Morocco.

The ecological and geographical diversity within Roman Africa is striking. In the east of the region it ranges from the pre-desert in the south, through the olive producing Sahel region in Byzacena, to the hills and plains of the Medjerda valley (the ancient Bagradas) that supported large-scale grain production. Along the northern coast of Tunisia and Algeria a series of mountain ranges come very close to the sea but are penetrated by rivers that give access into the interior and eventually the high plateau of Numidia and further mountain ranges such as the Aurès. Rainfall varies wildly. In the coastal mountains rainfall can be around 1200mm per annum whereas in the pre-desert, at the limit of Roman occupation, the total is much closer to 200mm. Agricultural produce, for which Africa was famous, varied correspondingly. In the north, along the Bagradas and on the coastal plain, cereals and vines dominated. Further south in Byzacena and on the high plateau olives and barley predominated (Mattingly 1988a: 44–9). Pastoral economies played a significant part in the economies of the mountains and pre-desert.

The control of transhumance across the Roman frontier and within Roman Africa seems to have been the main reason for the construction of the *fossatum* (a series of walls, ditches and forts) in the south of Africa Proconsularis and Numidia rather than to mark out the limit of Roman territory (Whittaker 1997: 47–8, 79–81; Shaw 1983: 137–8). The relationship between the tribes, settled communities and the Roman authorities was a source of tension throughout the period. Ecological conditions and the availability of agricultural land meant that urban settlements were not spread equally across Africa. There were particular concentrations of cities along the Bagradas and the coastal plains. The high plateau was less intensively urbanised than the coast, although there were many cities there. As might be expected, there were few cities on the borders of the pre-desert. Disparities in the extent of urban civilisation play a part in the nature and effect of that urban civilisation in Africa.

An important aspect of this book will be the brief evaluation of Carthaginian and Numidian urbanism. Many of the most prominent cities, especially those on the

Mediterranean coast, had pre-Roman origins and populations which affected their development for centuries after the Roman conquest. In reality the pre-Roman city deserves as much space as the Roman city but the focus of the book and the constraints of space preclude this. Examining the relationship between pre-Roman and Roman civilisations will be crucial to any understanding of the Romano-African city; for historical reasons this is fraught with difficulty. In the past an opposition has been set up between a Romanised elite and underlying resistance maintained by some Africans to imperial rule and culture (e.g. Frend 1952; Bénabou 1976; Laroui 1977). For such a conception the African city was just one of the battlegrounds over which cultural and occasionally real warfare was played out; tensions between the ruled and the rulers might be expected to have physical expression in the buildings of the region's cities. Such interpretations of the African experience under Rome were the product of historians of the post-colonial period reacting to earlier works that portrayed the African populations as passive receivers of superior Roman culture and which downplayed considerable non-Roman input. Archaeologists and historians of the late nineteenth- and early twentieth-century interpretations of the evidence were influenced by colonial propaganda and justifications (Mattingly 1996: 50–7). France and Italy were the new Rome dealing with a less civilised Africa. For instance, Broughton argued that: 'Here [in the Sahel] the French by following Roman methods are making the country prosperous once more', whilst Chatelain claimed the French, as the descendants of the Romans, had more right to the land than '*les Arabes*' (Broughton 1929: 4; Chatelain 1918: 4). Achievements in the past were Roman, modern achievements were European; natives were written out or characterised as savages: 'It is doubtful even if they had remained untouched by foreign influences if they would have evolved any advanced political or social organization.' (Broughton 1929: 6) Although distasteful to modern eyes, these views were influenced by contemporary society; historians and archaeologists are not divorced from their own socio-political milieu.

In correctly challenging earlier preconceptions about the process of Romanisation as a top-down imposition of a superior culture, post-colonialist and Marxist historians created an overly neat dichotomy between those citizens of Africa who were Romans by ancestry, or Romanised natives, the elite, and those who were resistors (Bénabou 1976; Laroui 1977; some elements of which are criticised by Whittaker 1978b among others). For instance, Laroui's history dealing with the motives of colonial historians is, in itself, schematised and fails to truly come to grips with the ancient texts and their difficulties. As we shall see the population was much more diverse, with many more different groups and identities, than a split between Romans and non-Romans implies. In consequence there were many different reasons for adopting, and ways to adopt, elements of Roman architectural or monumental style or content. Assessing the relationship between non-Roman and Roman in terms of religion, entertainment, intellectual life, political and social cohesion will help to explain the structures that were created in the region's cities.

The material that can be used to examine the evolution of urbanism within Africa is vast and varied. There is a wealth of literary material from the region but its distribution across time, space and subject is not consistent. Roman history was the history of the emperor, the court, the senate and warfare. As such Africa was conceptually on the periphery of the Empire and unless an emperor travelled there, which was rare, or there was a war or rebellion, the historians of the period largely ignore it. Once Christians started to write letters and treatises the situation improves but again many sectors of the population are ignored and the focus is rarely on the city itself or the population's motives for creating specific types of structures. So, while the student of late Roman African religion is extremely well served by the preservation of hundreds of Bishop Augustine of Hippo Regius' letters, sermons and tracts, his writings tell us little, for example, about the African elite's motives for constructing monumental structures.

Inscriptions will be an important source for much of the imperial period as Roman Africans invested heavily in the 'epigraphic habit', the trend in certain regions, at certain times, to commemorate the construction of buildings, the careers of officials and the lives of the dead, by inscribing on stone (MacMullen 1982: 233–46). Inscriptions are particularly useful for the current study as they help to date monuments, allowing historians to analyse trends in building, the costs of building and even the reasons for construction. Just as with literary material, inscriptions are limited in that they tell us little about the lower classes and concentrate on the activities and motivations of the elite. The movement of inscriptions from their original locations in the late and post-Roman periods as earlier monuments were reused by the community decontextualises and reduces the information that we glean from them. When assessing the progress of urbanisation this need not be a major problem; inscriptions can be used to show the construction rates of certain types of monuments, and the motivations for construction may be apparent, even if we are not exactly certain what the inscription relates to. What they are less good at demonstrating is the social and cultural motivations behind a building's construction.

Archaeological evidence allows the historian to engage with a city's elites and general population in a way that other evidence does not; excavation of poorer housing can give a voice to these people. Archaeological evidence is not a panacea that can totally mitigate the biases produced by other evidence types. As has already been noted, archaeology is interpretative, with the preconceptions of the interpreter having an effect on the conclusions derived from the material. For instance, as both Février and Dunbabin have noted, the third century AD and the Vandal period (after AD 439) have had relatively few mosaics assigned to them partly because archaeologists have assumed that political crises created economic and social crises, so examples that could have been dated to those periods are pushed earlier or later to suit the specialists' own biases (Février 1982b: 829; Dunbabin 1978: 30–7). The study of African cities is also complicated by the fact that much of our archaeological evidence comes from excavations undertaken in the nineteenth and early twentieth centuries. Early archaeologists were not overly bothered by a stratigraphic examination of the remains, the concern was to excavate down to impressive mosaics or marble floors rather than to record earlier or later, perhaps less impressive, phases of occupation (the problems that this caused were recognised as early as the 1950s – Frend 1952: xv).

In consequence late Roman, Carthaginian, Numidian and Republican levels may not have been examined with the care that is necessary. Pottery sherds, almost indestructible, found in great quantities across Roman cities, and invaluable for their potential to date remains, were not the primary concern of pre-war archaeologists.

A perfect example of some of the problems with the archaeological material can be seen at Thamugadi (Ballu 1897; 1903; 1911). The city was excavated between the late nineteenth and early twentieth centuries and the excavated city plan demonstrates that a very large part of the city was revealed in less than 20 years; stratigraphy was not recorded and the reports lack enough detail to re-evaluate the data effectively. Only the inscriptions and mosaics allow the historian to begin to reconstruct the evolution of the city. It could be argued that at least the majority of the city plan has been revealed, but the question that could be asked then is: the city plan of what era? The stone-built buildings have been preserved, including churches, so we might argue that it represents the early fifth-century city, but not knowing enough about late Roman levels in many of the buildings it is difficult to be sure. Despite all of the problems of assessing disparate evidence types, an evaluation of African cities under the Roman Empire remains blessed with a wide range of material which can be investigated to answer the questions addressed in this book.

The book is largely organised chronologically. After a brief examination of the pre-Roman city (Chapter 1) it will examine 'Roman' cities in the later first century BC and the first century AD (Chapter 2), including the building of Roman colonies and the beginnings of new monumental building traditions, before examining the apogee of African urbanism in the second century, the 'written city', the use of statuary and the burgeoning construction of places for business, social display and entertainment (Chapter 4). Chapter 3 will examine religious life across the first few centuries AD, a key part of the lived experience of urban inhabitants and crucial for the understanding of the function of the Roman city. Chapter 5 will examine the building boom during the reign of the Severan emperors in the late second to early third centuries. Chapters 6 and 7 will examine developments to cities in the third and fourth centuries, including the effect of Christians on the cities of the region. The Emperor Constantine's conversion in around 312 had enduring consequences for Roman civilisation and there is a plethora of evidence to demonstrate the scope and scale of Christianity's impact. The concluding chapter will draw together themes in the book and will examine the nature of Roman-African urban civilisation.

I

The Numidian & Carthaginian Background

Introduction

The Romans did not occupy an empty landscape in Africa. Instead they conquered a region that contained distinct ethnic and political groupings and that displayed diversity in the population's use and approach to urbanism. This chapter will examine the formation and nature of these urban settlements as important phases of the development of African cities and urban culture. I will not catalogue the wars between Carthage and Rome, as their detail is not important for the current study and there are many books on the conflict. In terms of terminology 'Phoenician' refers to the cultures of Phoenicia and Phoenician colonies; 'Punic' can describe the cultures of the Phoenician colonies and others culturally influenced by them; 'Carthaginian' refers to the people and culture of the city of Carthage and, increasingly from the fifth century BC, the term can be used to imply some form of hegemonic control over other Punic cities, then parts of Africa and Spain (Ben Younes 1995: 820–1).

Historians who assess the development and character of Numidian and Carthaginian cities during the first millennium BC are reliant on archaeological material. The relevant literary material was produced by Romans or Greeks who tended to categorise these civilisations as either 'the enemy' or 'barbarians' depending on time, place and context, which undoubtedly led to the distortion of reality (Laroui 1977: 28). Additionally extant writings mainly post-date the defeat of Carthage by Rome and are rarely concerned, and never in any systematic way, with urban culture. The historian must therefore combine the considerable body of archaeological material with the scanty literary evidence to build a complex picture of the evolution of first-millennium BC urban society.

Greek and Roman geographers and historians used a wide range of terminology to define the 'native' populations of Africa. Some early definitions were to be perpetuated in the Greco-Roman historical tradition because of the failure to recognise change and the tendency to use earlier terminology to explain current realities. Herodotus, the first Greek historian, used the general description of 'Libyan' to apply to all of the tribes in these regions (Herodotus, *Histories*, 4.168.1). He then specified individual tribes and gave their domains, with descriptions becoming more fanciful the further west and away from the coast they were supposed to be located (Herodotus, *Histories*, 4.168–85). Later, when the Romans began to interact with these people, the tribes in what came to be Mauretania were often grouped together as Mauri and from the Second Punic War onwards those in Numidia and Proconsularis as Numidians, although 'Libyan' could still be used. To the south were the tribes of the Gaetulians and Garamantes. Some modern historians have defined all these groups as the ancestors of the Berbers on the basis of linguistics and the current territorial distribution of modern Berber peoples; the term has also been used as a weapon in nationalistic agendas during the post-colonial debates on the Roman world (Frend 1952; Thébert 1978; Bénabou 1978; Brett & Fentress 1996: 1–6. The latter uses the word in terms of linguistics but argues against a cultural definition of Berber for the past). Bénabou has argued that if 'berberism' has been used for *'causes douteuses'* (doubtful causes) in the past that is no reason to deprive the people of Africa the name of Berber, but such a link is dangerous (Bénabou 1978: 84). Pre-Roman populations may be a large part of the ancestors of modern Berbers and their languages are derived, in part, from languages spoken in pre-Roman times. However, the term fails to take into account population movements that added Phoenicians, Romans, Jews and Arabs to the ethnic mix of the region. Furthermore, 'Berber' derives from the same root as 'barbarian' – people who were not Greek and instead made unintelligible *bar, bar* noises; it was a term of abuse. This book will therefore avoid 'Berber' as being loaded with cultural preconceptions and will instead use 'Libyan' or more specific tribal names.

The Coming of the Phoenicians

By the late eighth century BC Libyan peoples were living in both settled and nomadic communities across northern Africa as far as Egypt. Some of these may have been nucleated in some way but it was into a largely non-urban world that the Phoenicians established their first African colonies. The end of the second millennium BC probably marks the beginning of Phoenician maritime commercial exploration but we are ill-served by the ancient sources when we wish to analyse the dating and causes of colonisation. The literary material is largely silent on causation and when foundation dates are recorded they are steeped in myth. The Phoenicians, from city-states in what is now coastal Syria and Lebanon, were thought by ancient writers, perhaps based on Punic legends or records, to have founded Gades (Cadiz) in Spain in 1110 BC and Utica in 1101 BC; Lixus supposedly ante-dated Gades (Pliny, *H.N.* 29.63; 16.216; Velleius Paterculus 1.2.3, 6.4; Map 1). Most sources claim that settlers from Tyre founded Carthage in 814/3.

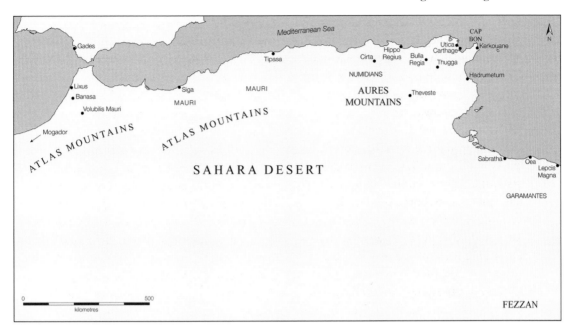

Map 1 Punic and Numidian cities.

Corroborating the literary evidence with archaeological remains is extremely problematic as there is little physical evidence for these Phoenician colonies before the mid-late eighth century BC. If we take Carthage as an example, until very recently despite the best efforts of some archaeologists the earliest burials at the city, which constitute all our evidence for the earliest city, never pre-dated the second half of the eight century BC, casting doubt on the traditional foundation date. New bone samples, however, from one cemetery at Carthage have been dated to the late ninth century on the basis of radiocarbon dating, which could be said to confirm the legendary date (Quinn 2009: 263–4). This is, however, a very small amount of material on which to base an argument and, in any case, the presence of some burials in the area dated to the late ninth century does not necessarily mean that the deceased were colonists; they could have been traders or locals. This problem of interpretation applies to many isolated finds of early Phoenician goods in Africa and Spain. In the earliest periods, when there is little settlement or burial evidence, we can suspect trade rather than colonisation being behind the presence of the material. It is also possible that seasonal marketplaces and emporia may subsequently have become colonies, complicating the debate further. Later local populations might have adopted Phoenician goods and practices again, appearing as colonists rather than locals.

Trade and the acquisition of goods not being easily available in the Phoenician homeland was undoubtedly a key motive for exploration and colonisation. Archaeological evidence from sites in southern Spain, for example Gades, points to a Phoenician presence there by the eighth century, although many sites were relatively small (*c.*10ha or less) until the sixth century (Aubet 1995: 55–6). These Spanish sites were close to sources of metals that were in demand elsewhere in the Mediterranean (Strabo, *Geography*, 3.2.9–11). Gradually cities were established in the south of Spain, along the Mediterranean coast of North Africa, in western Sicily, on Sardinia, Corsica and Malta or beyond the Pillars of Hercules on the African Atlantic. Some settlements may have initially been stepping stones to the Spanish settlements, rather than deliberate acts of colonisation. Such Phoenician enterprises, like contemporary Greek colonies, would also have acted as a valve to release population pressures at home. The formation of a large continental empire does not appear to have been a preoccupation of the colonisers and given that we are seeing the work of the populations of a series of Phoenician city-states over a considerable time span, we should not expect the colonies to be part of a coherent plan.

Whatever the specific reasons for the implantation of a colony, it is clear that their locations, as new homes for non-native populations a long way from home, and their later evolution, was affected by their nature. Colonists needed to make decisions about how they would balance access to resources and trade with defence. The colonies were established on or very near the coast on easily defendable islands or quasi-islands. Gades, Motya, off Sicily, and Mogador, a seasonal trading station on Africa's Atlantic coast, were on islands (Lancel 1995b: 12–3; Jodin 1966: 192). Utica was on a defendable promontory overlooking the sea at the mouth of a river (Lancel 1995a: 374; Lancel 1995b: 17). Carthage and its immediate territory were less connected to the rest of Tunisia than it is today. Pre-Roman Tipasa was sited on a promontory with potential harbours on either side (Lancel 1995b: 96). This should not be a surprise to us: maritime trade, the probable raison d'être of many of these sites, conditioned the settlers to locate their colony close to the sea while an easily defendable site on an island, or with a convenient hill refuge nearby, was necessary in case of attack. The strategic concerns of Phoenician colonists were echoed by the populations of Greek colonies. The city of Cyrene in Cyrenaica, to the east of our study area, for instance, swapped being situated on the sea with a location that guaranteed security and plentiful rainfall (Herodotus, *Histories*, 4.153–8).

Carthage

Carthage's eventual dominance among the Phoenician colonies was partly due to its position on east–west and north–south Mediterranean trade routes; its location and commercial activities clearly helped to expand its economy and therefore its ability to fund a powerful military. The extent to which Carthage used this wealth and military power to create an empire has been much debated. When did Carthage cease to be just one of many colonies, becoming first hegemonic over the other Phoenician cities and then, eventually, an imperial power? Also, what effect did this have on urban development at other sites? Understanding the process is difficult but it seems to be marked by a gradual acquisition of territory and influence. We are ill-served in analysing these problems by the ancient sources. For instance, the

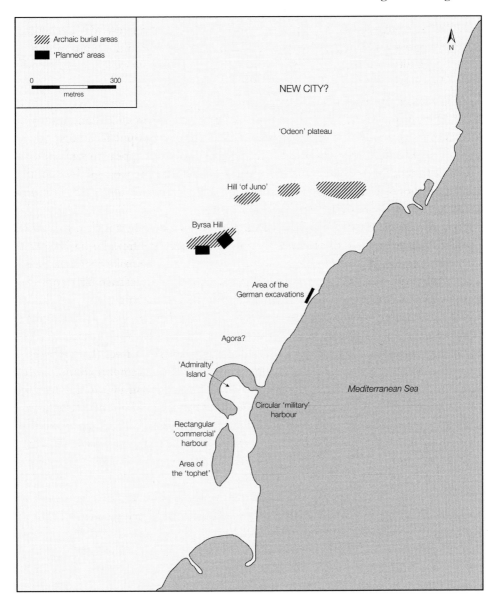

Fig. 1.1 Punic Carthage: after Ennabli 1997: 6.

abandonment of some sites in Sardinia in the sixth century has been presented as being the consequence of Carthaginian action (Aubet 1995: 48), but in general our understanding of the process is hampered by a tendency in the Greek and Roman sources to conflate Carthaginian, Punic and Phoenician. So from the wars on Sicily in the sixth century onwards, the Carthaginians are always presented as being the driving force behind the Phoenician colonies (Whittaker 1978a). This may well be due to a lack of Greco-Roman understanding of internal Punic politics or anachronism in our sources. In other areas Carthaginian dominance may have taken rather longer to develop and may have been a consequence of the Phoenician Sicilian colonies becoming dependent on Carthage's aid against Syracuse and other Greek cities. From the fourth century onwards, Carthage was the most powerful Punic city practising regional hegemony over Punic communities and, from the fourth century in Africa and the mid-third century in Spain, it began to acquire a continental empire. So we have a very gradual acquisition of territory and influence. Within Africa there is little to suggest that a city such as Utica was directly governed by Carthage, although allied cities were certainly capable of being alienated from Carthage; many cities, including Tunis, rebelled during the Mercenary War, and Utica and other major cities abandoned Carthage during the Third Punic War (Polybius, *Histories*, 1.66–78; Appian, *Libyca*, 94).

As stated above the earliest archaeological evidence from Carthage comes from graves. Tombs of the late eighth and early seventh centuries, and perhaps also of the late ninth century, helped to define the boundaries of the earliest city (Lancel 1982: 357–9; Quinn 2009: 264). The tombs have been found on the Byrsa hill, the Hill of Juno and across to Dermech, and their position above a narrow plain and the sea seems to indicate that the earliest settlement is likely to have been found on that plain. Other Punic cities placed their burial grounds at the edges of the urban area or even on nearby islands (Lancel 1995a: 377). For instance, the island colony of Motya, off Sicily, had burial grounds at the northern edge of the island but also on the nearby coast, while Kerkouane had its necropolis some distance from the city (Whitaker 1921: 206, 231; Lancel 1995a: 380). These arrangements express a key Mediterranean ideology about the relationship between the living and the dead; ritual pollution accompanied the dead and they were to be kept beyond the bounds of the city.

To the south of early Carthage was the '*tophet*', an open-air sacred enclosure dedicated to the god Baal Hammon and containing cremation burials of children and votive deposits of small animals and birds. Initially the *tophet* contained a 'chapel' that was later abandoned and had votive deposits placed around it (Picard 1954: 32–3; Lancel 1995b: 27–32; 227–48). By the fifth to fourth centuries it also contained stelae that are identified as being in honour of the city's principal goddess Tanit (Bénichou-Safar 2004: 83; see Chapter 3; Fig. 1.2). It has usually been dated, on the basis of Greek pottery, from the second half of the eighth century BC to the fall of Carthage, although Bénichou-Safar argues that a date around 800 BC can be supported by comparing Phoenician pottery in the *tophet* and the Near East (Lancel 1995c: 26–7; Bénichou-Safar 2004: 121–9). The argument relies on relatively limited archaeological evidence though and the traditional dating remains better supported.

The *tophet* has been at the centre of debates about human and particularly child sacrifice in the Punic world, with some seeing the cremations as being the physical evidence for children being sacrificed to the gods. This is not the place to rehearse those inconclusive arguments (Lancel 1995b: 227–56 sensibly concludes that the problem is 'insoluble') again, except to say that nothing at the *tophets* of Carthage and other Punic sites prevents them being cemeteries dedicated to children (a not uncommon cross-cultural phenomenon), an interpretation supported by a relative

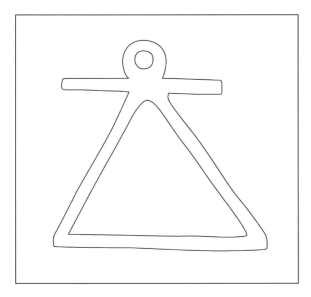

Fig. 1.2 Generic Sign of Tanit.

lack of child burial elsewhere at Carthage (Bénichou-Safar 2004: 121–9). The literary material that suggests human sacrifice is extremely untrustworthy because of the
Greco-Roman sources' (e.g. Diodorus 20.14) hostility to Carthage and because the
Biblical sources (e.g. II Kings 3.27, 16.3, 21.6) are actually writing in the main about
practices within Israel and neighbouring states rather than in the Punic world itself.

Carthage gradually developed on the coastal plain and the hills to the west; this
area remained the heart of the city until its destruction by Rome. The early Punic
city is not well understood because of the impact of Roman and modern settlement,
but there are indications that there was orthogonal (roads meeting at right angles)
planning on the coast from the eighth century BC onwards (Niemeyer 1992: 39–41;
Ben Younes 1995: 824–5). Over time the city expanded, and in the fifth century the
burial area on the hill of Juno was impinged on by housing; the same may also be
true of other areas although often it was initially artisan and industrial workshops that
first invaded the necropoleis (Lancel 1995b: 135–40). Some of these burial zones had
probably ceased to be operational by the time that they were incorporated and built
over, but other necropoleis were surrounded and embedded in the urban topography
(Lancel 1995a: 378). By the fifth century at the latest, the city was ringed with an
impressive set of walls that were added to and expanded on over time.

The narrow coastal plain may have been an impediment to city growth as in the
fifth century the population reclaimed land from the sea. A wall and sea-gate discovered by a German archaeological mission shows breakwater blocks being put in place
to increase the available land for construction (Rakob 1992: 34). There also seems
to have been an urban, or perhaps suburban, area north of the cemeteries. Some
occupation levels have been discovered there and there are a few difficult to interpret
hints in the literary material that suggest a 'new city' away from the coastal plain
(Lancel 1995b: 141–2). The extent and nature of the city is unclear, not least because
Carthage's Phoenician name, Qart Hadasht, also meant 'new city'. By the fifth to

third centuries BC there was a system of regularly planned radiating roads on the eastern side of the Byrsa hill that followed its contours. The roads of this quarter were not paved but were composed of beaten earth, which would have stood up to most environmental conditions and could have been re-laid if it became heavily rutted (Lancel 1995a: 386). The orthogonal plan of the coastal plain remained intact. So in the mid-Punic period there were two different systems of planning in different parts of Carthage that responded to the needs of the population. The dual evolution neatly dealt with the problems of terrain but also the need to navigate around the city.

Despite Carthage's defeat by Rome in the First and Second Punic Wars (264–241; 218–201) and the levying of huge fines against the city, Carthage actually seems to have attained its greatest extent during the second century BC. On the face of it, development in the second century BC would seem to be surprising. At the end of the Second Punic War the city lost its domains outside of north-eastern Tunisia as well as access to the mines of south-eastern Spain, which had become a Roman province. However, the treaty of 201 allowed Carthage to keep its mercantile fleet and the best agricultural land in north-western Africa. Additionally, with the end of the Second Punic War wasteful military expenditure was reduced which will have allowed the populace to focus on improving their urban environment. Carthage's immense wealth in this period can be demonstrated by its offer to pay off its fine 40 years early in 191 and its ability to export grain to Rome during the first half of the second century BC (Livy 36.4.7–9; 31.19.2). A series of excavations undertaken as part of the Save Carthage Campaign in the 1970s and 1980s revealed city expansion and monumental changes in the course of that century. New housing areas were created in the area to the south of the Byrsa hill and there was slight expansion on the eastern coastline (Lancel & Morel 1992: 47–53; Rakob 1992: 34). The slight advance towards the coast detected in the German excavation also showed richer houses, arranged around peristyle (colonnaded) courtyards, which replaced the previous simple housing blocks (Rakob 1992: 33). These various excavations demonstrate the variety of housing in the city, which were paralleled elsewhere in the Punic world. We also know that tower blocks were present at Phoenician-Punic cities. Motya and Tyre were both described as having tall buildings by classical authors and Carthage also had apartment blocks in the region of the Byrsa (Strabo, *Geography*, 16.2.23; Appian, *Libyca*, 128). The German excavations also showed second century alterations to the city walls with a gate being removed.

Without going into comprehensive detail about the city in the Carthaginian period, it is important to note that it also had an *agora*, an open space for markets and political meetings, libraries which, according to Pliny the Elder, were shared out between the Numidian kings following Carthage's destruction, and at least two temples, which will be discussed in more detail later (Pliny, *H.N.*, 17.22–3; Appian, *Libyca*, 127, 130), by the time of its destruction. All of these building types will be seen in later Roman cities.

During the second century BC a major infrastructure project was undertaken to improve Carthage's commercial installations. Two large harbours were carved out inland from the coast in the south of the city and connected to the sea by a channel (Lancel 1995b: 182–8). This *cothon*, as the Greco-Roman sources call it, had two elements to it, an outer rectangular commercial harbour and an inner circular military harbour. The military harbour had an artificial island in the centre to give the fleet commander a view over the harbours and docks, and there were ship-sheds around the outside of the harbour; Appian states that there were places for 220 ships in the circular harbour (Appian, *Libyca*, 96). Appian's claim that the harbours were burnt during Carthage's destruction in the Third Punic War is confirmed by the presence of burnt layers of the second century AD (Hurst 1994: 17–8). Other Punic cities, such as Motya, had artificial harbours, but the Carthaginian anchorages dwarfed these.

Carthage should not be seen as an archetypal example of Punic urbanism. It was unique in its scale, wealth and culture, and we should not expect other cities to be identical. However, it was a model from which other settlements could copy and adapt cultural elements.

Native 'Urbanism'

The creation of Phoenician colonies in the second half of the first millennium BC seems to have fuelled state formation among the native tribes. Perhaps under pressure exerted by Carthaginian expansionism into Africa, there was a process of state formation so that large kingdoms such as those of the Mauri, Masaesylii and Massylies, which incorporated many smaller tribes, begin to appear in the third century BC (Pliny, *H.N.*, 5.4.29–30). The reign of Massinissa, King of the Massylies from 206 to 148 BC is important in the development of the Numidian kingdom. Having sided with the Romans in the Second and Third Punic Wars, he benefited through the acquisition of territory from both the Carthaginians and Numidian rivals who had chosen the wrong side. From the end of the Second Punic War in 201 we can talk about a Numidian kingdom and from the end of the second century two Mauretanian kingdoms. The formation of larger more centralised states also led to the formation of some urban centres in Numidian territory, although these remained relatively limited until the last century BC. We should therefore be suspicious of the model of outsiders bringing culture to 'backward' Africans. For instance, when Phoenician traders were looking to establish markets in North Africa it seems that in Mauretania they made use of pre-existing settlements (Saint-Amans 2004: 38). The benefits for the traders are obvious. Existing nucleated settlements would have already functioned as markets and would have been known to be receptive to trade anyway. Trading, rather than the creation of new colonies, would naturally have focused on such places. Whether such settlements can truly be considered 'urban' is harder to know.

Other urban developments took place at some distance from the Phoenician colonies. For instance, in the proto-historic period (1000–500 BC) the tribe of the Garamantes, located in a series of wadis (seasonal river valleys) in the Fazzan area to the south of what became Tripolitania, had many nucleated settlements of different types (Daniels 1989: 45–61). These sites had wide 'cemetery' zones with burials placed into individual funerary monuments (Mattingly 2007: 140–1). Zinchecra, an early promontory fort defended by a wall with hut complexes inside, has provided evidence of many different types of cultivated cereal and fruit crops but perhaps was not a truly urban site (Van Der Veen 1992: 12). Later Garamantian towns, such as the capital Germa, close to Zinchecra, remained outside Carthaginian and Roman control, which is not to say that the civilisation was not affected by cultural and trade contacts with the coastal civilisations, but it was mediated in a less direct manner (see Mattingly 1995: 33–6). Occasional Roman expeditions into Garamantian territory and Garamantian ambassadors to Rome demonstrate the cultural links and the potential for the transfer of Roman ideas beyond the frontier (Daniels 1989: 45; Pliny, *H.N.*, 5.43–6).

Urban sites, in closer proximity to Carthaginian influence, appear in the literary sources and in the archaeological records from the fourth century BC onwards. One of the earliest to appear in the literature is a Numidian city called by the Greek name Hecatompylos, meaning 'hundred-gated' and presumably a translation of a Punic or Numidian name. The city is only mentioned in passing in connection with the activities of the Carthaginian general Hanno, who seized it in 247 BC, and there are few indications of its buildings or character in the texts, but 'hundred-gated' implies that it was a very large city (Diodorus 4.18.1; 24.10.2; Polybius, *Histories*, 1.73.1). Desanges and Lancel believed that Hecatompylos and the later Roman city of Theveste were, in all likelihood, the same town (Desanges 1978: 187; Lancel 1995b: 259 – 'must be'; against – Fentress 1979: 32–3). However, as there are no useful geographical indications as to where Hecatompylos was located in Polybius and Diodorus, it would be inappropriate to use Theveste's archaeology to inform Hecatompylos' history.

'Punic' Urbanism

Colonisation from Carthage has been hypothesised for several settlements in Africa and beyond, in particular for the coastal emporia of Sabratha, Oea (modern Tripoli) and Lepcis Magna in coastal Tripolitania. The former two cities seem to have been originally seasonal, with layers of sand alternating with occupation debris in their very earliest incarnations; the first stone buildings were established in the mid-fourth century BC although ancient Oea is badly known due to its permanence of settlement into the modern era (Dore 1988: 74; Mattingly 1995: 123–6). Lepcis Magna, on the other hand, has a very substantial structure, probably a public building, near the Mediterranean coast to the north of the *forum vetus* (old forum) of the Roman period (the Roman equivalent of the *agora*). Built at some stage in the late seventh to sixth century BC, the building lay just inside what has been interpreted as a city wall (Carter 1965: 125–6, 131). Given the early date of foundation, the excavators proposed that the city was originally colonised directly from Phoenicia, later becoming tributary to Carthage (Carter 1965: 131; Livy 34.62). Proof for this hypothesis is lacking, although

Longerstay argues that it is supported by religious practice, as the Lepcitanian population seems to have emphasised different deities to that of Carthage (Longerstay 1995: 843; Di Vita, on the other hand, views the city as being an emporia of Carthage – Di Vita 1982: 516). The patron deities of Lepcis were Milk'Ashtart and Shadrapa, who had temples in Lepcis' *forum vetus* by the first century BC; Shadrapa appears to be a saviour/fertility deity whilst Milk'Ashtart is the 'king' of the city (the *mlk* element means 'king' in Phoenician/Punic). Lepcis also preserves many inscriptions to Astarte, a key goddess in the Phoenician pantheon. The Carthaginian favourites Baal Hammon and Tanit are, however, largely absent from Lepcis apart from the 'Sign of Tanit' appearing on amphorae in tombs. Lepcis' religion and possibly its foundation seem then to be unmediated by the influence of Carthage but it would only take the discovery of an inscription or temple to change the picture markedly.

After the Second Punic War literary and archaeological evidence suggests that Massinissa had several urban centres scattered throughout his kingdom. Cirta, Zama Regia, Bulla Regia, Hippo Regius are all mentioned as being cities of the Numidian kingdom, whilst to the west in the Mauretanian kingdom there were a few cities, such as Volubilis or Siga (Berthier 1980: 19–26; Brett and Fentress 1996: 32; Jodin 1987: 33–57). Even if we add in those cities that are known from archaeology, such as Thugga or Banasa, this is not a great many locations; clearly large tracts of the kingdom must have remained rural (Girard 1984: 11–93). These Numidian cities, their function, their architecture and even their populace, had clearly been affected by the proximity of the Carthage and the Punic cities. Niemeyer (1995: 264) argues that it is difficult to tell the difference between a Phoenician/Carthaginian city and a Numidian Punicised city in terms of its layout and the types of habitations and religious structure present, although it might be argued that the presence of specific tomb types or deities might be diagnostic. To complicate matters, at many sites in Numidia urbanism becomes perceptible only when they came under Carthage's power or influence (Saint-Amans 2004: 17); although this may just reflect the interests of archaeologists who have not concentrated on excavating pre-Roman remains. Goods, even whole assemblies of goods, and names are not necessarily diagnostic of the ethnic origins of a population, but clearly there was a movement of ideas from Carthage to other groups. This process of acculturation was not an imposition of a dominant culture on to Numidian tribes, but rather the movement of ideas between peoples are the product of a dialogue. Groups who adopt new ways of doing things from outside are not likely to take on ideas wholesale without adapting them in some way so that they are useful within their own culture (Ben Younes 2007: 32–4; Stone 2007: 46–9). New ideas helped to enrich aspects of native culture such as funerary rites or building types, they did not replace fundamental beliefs (Ben Younes 1995: 823–4). Numidian populations who used aspects of foreign cultures, for instance the Punic language or urban planning, were not adopting all aspects of Carthaginian life but were interpreting useful elements of other societies in their own way.

Thugga is a good example of a Numidian/Punic city whose population was using some cultural elements from the Carthaginians, as well as from the wider Hellenised

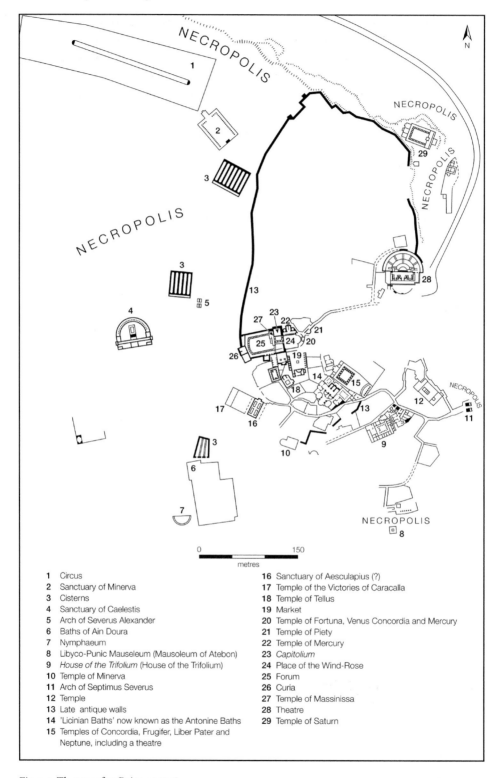

Fig. 1.3 Thugga: after Poinssot 1958.

1	Circus	16	Sanctuary of Aesculapius (?)
2	Sanctuary of Minerva	17	Temple of the Victories of Caracalla
3	Cisterns	18	Temple of Tellus
4	Sanctuary of Caelestis	19	Market
5	Arch of Severus Alexander	20	Temple of Fortuna, Venus Concordia and Mercury
6	Baths of Ain Doura	21	Temple of Piety
7	Nymphaeum	22	Temple of Mercury
8	Libyco-Punic Mauseleum (Mausoleum of Atebon)	23	*Capitolium*
9	*House of the Trifolium* (House of the Trifolium)	24	Place of the Wind-Rose
10	Temple of Minerva	25	Forum
11	Arch of Septimus Severus	26	Curia
12	Temple	27	Temple of Massinissa
13	Late antique walls	28	Theatre
14	'Licinian Baths' now known as the Antonine Baths	29	Temple of Saturn
15	Temples of Concordia, Frugifer, Liber Pater and Neptune, including a theatre		

culture of the Mediterranean and Egypt, to express status and power in the second century BC. The city, built on a plateau and slope with a ravine on one side, is likely to have been under direct Carthaginian control from the fourth century BC onwards (Lancel 1995b: 263). During the invasion of Agathocles, tyrant of Syracuse in 310–307 BC, the city could be described as 'large' but what that actually means is difficult to define (Diodorus 20.57.4). It is unlikely that the pre-Roman city was any larger than the later Roman city, which probably had a population of no more than 10,000 people (Duncan-Jones 1963: 89). After Carthage's defeat in the Second Punic War the city became one centre of the Numidian kingdom and the surviving pre-Roman structures date to this period.

There is comparatively little evidence about habitation at the site in the pre-Roman period, although that is starting to change, and instead most evidence of urban life comes from the spheres of religion, burial and monumental building. The ethnicity of the population is difficult to define (Khanoussi et al. 2004–05: 52–8). One of the few Punic inscriptions from the site comes from the monument (or temple) to the Numidian King Massinissa at Thugga (Brett & Fentress 1996; Saint-Amans 2004: 46–9). The text, dated to 138 BC, shows individuals with Punic names at the city, for example Hanno and Iatonbaal, but given Carthaginian dominance in the region before the Second Punic War it would not be surprising if local families had adopted Carthaginian names (see Chapter 2 for similar processes under Rome). The inscription also demonstrates the complexity of the town's organisation. Several officials and positions are designated, often by the Libyan term GLD, which means chief or ruler, but what it means precisely in the context of Thugga is unclear. The structure to Massinissa was located near a paved area, apparently a central square, which lay underneath the later Roman forum (Saint-Amans 2004: 44–6). The presence of the Numidian 'forum' on a site that would become the juridical, governmental and ritual focus of the Roman town again implies substantial central organisation at Thugga in the pre-Roman period, as well as continuity into the Roman period.

Thugga's dolmen necropolis to the north of the site also testifies to first-millennium BC occupation, although exact dates are not clear (Poinssot 1958: 9). That the cemetery continued in use into the second century AD points to some continuity in burial ideology among the populace from pre-Carthaginian to Roman times. The best-known burial monument at the city, the mausoleum of Ateban, son of Iepmatah (note the Numidian names), dates from the second century BC and displays a different set of artistic and cultural values than the dolmens. A range of cultures influenced the style of the monument and presumably the town as well. Egyptian and Hellenistic elements, also seen in second-century BC mausolea at Sabratha and the monumental tumulus of the Medracen, are present in the structure's design with Greek elements – column capitals, scenes with horse-drawn chariots, statues of sirens – being melded with the Egyptian – mouldings, lotus leaf capitals and a pyramid topping the edifice (Poinssot 1958: 58–9; Lancel 1995b: 308–9; Picard 1954: 33). The individuals who paid for its construction (whether the deceased, their family or a wider grouping of the elite) clearly wished to use artistic and architectural styles which keyed into the wider Hellenistic culture of the Mediterranean. By building a monument in this fashion the community, or parts of the community, were showing off their wealth and power and demonstrating that they understood sophisticated urban living.

Turning to religion, several different deities are honoured on stelae away from Carthage. For instance, Reshef and Baal Shamin are documented at Hadrumetum and Baal Addir is known from El-Hofra, where the earliest inscription is dated to 162 BC (Cintas 1947: 46; Berthier & Charlier 1955: 231); Hadrumetum's *tophet* was used from the seventh century BC to first century AD (Berthier & Charlier 1955: 222; Foucher 1964: 35–6). Open-air shrines to Punic or local deities were also very common into the Roman period, and Baal and his consort Tanit seem to have been worshipped in such structures (Le Glay 1966: 269–72). At Thugga an enclosure dedicated to Baal in the north-east of the site was constructed around the same time as the 'temple' to Massinissa and the mausoleum (Saint-Amans 2004: 351). Other similar sites in Africa also date from this period; for instance that at Sabratha dates to the second century BC and Gheran's origins were of the third century BC (Brouquier-Reddé 1992: 28–30). Such sanctuaries tended to be placed on the periphery of a city and were sometimes initially spatially divorced from it, although over time city expansion often incorporated them into the urban framework (Lancel 1995a: 381).

Some substantial temple buildings appear alongside the open-air sanctuaries. The accounts of the sack of Carthage by the Romans mention temples to Apollo and Aesculapius; probably these were dedicated to the Punic deities Reshef and Eschmoun respectively (Appian, *Libyca*, 127, 130; Livy 41.22, 42.24). There are also examples of temples at Cadiz, Ras Ed-Drek, Motya and Kerkouane to a range of deities (Picard 1954: 69; Lancel 1995a: 383; Pomponius Mela 3.6.46; Isserlin 1974: 96; Fantar 1987: 145–221; Cadotte 2007: 283). These temples often had a sacred area or *temenos* (enclosure) around them into which votive deposits and stelae were placed. The Cappiddazzu temple on Motya was slightly different. Whilst it had an open-air enclosure, its focus was a structure with three *cellae* (cult enclosures); such a set-up repeatedly appears in Roman Africa (Isserlin 1974: 96).

The mid-second century BC marks something of a cultural watershed for Thugga's population. Monumental building, cult places and inscriptions appear. All of these elements suggest that in the mid-second century BC Thugga was a truly urban site on the frontiers of Numidian and Carthaginian Africa. Thugga was not alone in this. Other native sites in the interior seem to have become more dynamic in this period. The geographer Strabo claimed that Massinissa had taught urbanism and agriculture to his people and it is tempting to argue that the indications of monumentalisation at Thugga and elsewhere in this period are concrete reflections of Strabo's information (Strabo, *Geography*, 17.3.15; Polybius, *Histories*, 37). However, what Strabo's sources for this statement are is unclear and there was a tendency in the ancient world to conflate societal and legal developments with strong, famous rulers. Massinissa may have encouraged urbanism and agriculture but we may doubt that he was solely responsible for its uptake, not least because of the examples of Zinchecra and Germa mentioned above. It must also be remembered that for much of Massinissa and his

Fig. 1.4 An orthogonally planned city, Priene: after Bayhan, S. 1997. *Priene, Miletus, Didyma*, Antalya: 13.

successors' reigns, Thugga was entirely atypical of most settlements throughout Numidia, which seem to have remained as villages.

We have already seen orthogonal planning at Carthage from an early date and the concept was becoming popular in the course of the third and second centuries BC in the cities of the Mediterranean coast, such as Lepcis, Sabratha and Tipasa (Saint-Amans 2004: 39; Fig. 2.1) and even inland at places such as Tamuda or Volubilis (Brett & Fentress 1996: 32). The main impetus for such arrangements had permeated out from the eastern Mediterranean from the fifth century onwards and was applied to

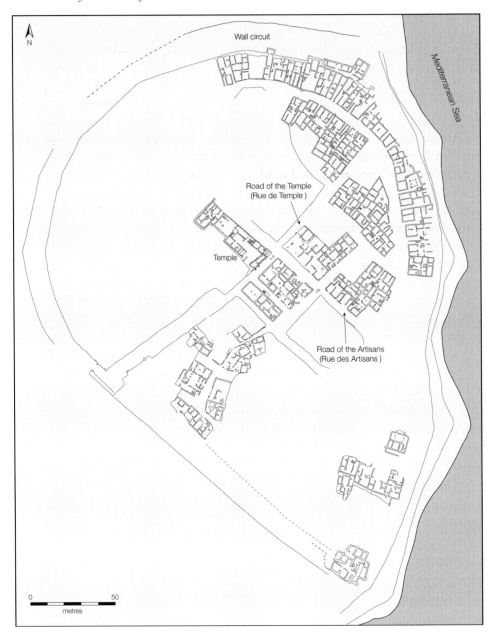

Fig. 1.5 Kerkouane: after Fantar 1987.

their settlements by populations in Spain, Italy and Africa. Pre-Roman Thugga and most other cities in the interior were not, however, planned on this neat right-angled grid. Instead they were oriented according to the natural contours of the site and to take into account the prevailing winds; the orthogonal layout was not always the best way to take into account geographical and meteorological elements despite being a rational way of organising a city.

A city such as fourth- and third-century BC Kerkouane demonstrates that local populations adapted aspects of Carthaginian culture in their own way. The city's inhabitants, under the influence of the metropolis only 70km away, recognised the benefits of Carthaginian town planning but did not adopt all elements of Carthaginian urban life. There was an ovoid external esplanade inside the city walls that provided the framework into which the rest of the roads, which as at Carthage were constructed of beaten earth, fitted. The roads 'of the artisans' and 'of the temple' provided the main roads of the small city, meeting at a crossroads roughly in its centre, with other streets being articulated around this nexus. There was clearly a concern to create an orthogonal area but the external road essentially undermined it and away from the centre it is clear that the grid structure was lost; where the urban framework was not useful to the inhabitants it was abandoned.

As at the later phases in Carthage, houses at Kerkouane were organised around courtyards but these were accessed from the street through long corridors; clearly privacy was an issue for the inhabitants. The courtyards were not as elaborate as many at Carthage, they were not always colonnaded and were not always regular quadrilaterals, but some owners had mosaic floors (Fantar 1987: 143). We should not expect that the quality of the housing at Kerkouane would be the same as that of Carthage, given that one was a metropolis and the other a provincial town. The Kerkouane houses do not seem to have had the cisterns that many Carthaginian habitations had, but they did have baths with incorporated seats in rooms that often opened off the courtyards, conduits draining excess water out into the streets (Lancel 1995b: 169–71; Fantar 1987: 100–1; Plate 2). This particular bath type is currently unparalleled at other sites, although various houses at Carthage seem to have wet-rooms created for ablutions (Thébert 2003: 64–5). There is little evidence in the pre-Roman period for public bathing installations. There are two buildings at Kerkouane that could possibly be bath houses but the evidence is slim (Thébert 2003: 57–8). The flowering of a powerful tradition of Romano-African bathing in the second to fourth centuries AD appears to have few links with any African pre-Roman custom (see Chapters 2, 4 and 7).

Pre-Roman Urbanism

By the time the first Roman province was created in Africa in 146 BC, in the aftermath of Carthage's destruction, there was already an urban tradition from Tripolitania to the Atlantic Ocean. Undoubtedly the greatest concentration of urban settlements was along the coast, in northern Tunisia and around Cirta in Numidia. It was in these areas that Punic influence had been the strongest, where native kingdoms with strong centralised authority had formed and where agriculture could easily support the creation of nucleated settlements and complicated governmental structures, whilst providing resources for the building of monumental constructions. Additionally, some urban life was being experienced deep into the pre-desert in the kingdom of the Garamantes; the creation of towns was not just in response to colonisation.

In the pre-Roman period organised orthogonal street grids, often containing a central *forum/agora* were common, although by no means universal; streets might be paved but might be of beaten earth. Coastal sites often built port structures and many cities were walled. Housing varied from city to city, although the house arranged around a peristyle courtyard was used at numerous sites. Sacred areas of different types were used by the African populations; temple buildings and structures that incorporated both a temple and open ground into which votive deposits were placed are all known. Additionally, there were open *tophet* areas for burial alongside dedications to deities. All of these elements of urban life were built on in the Roman period.

2

Urbanisation & Governance,
146 BC to AD 100

Conquering Africa

The Roman occupation of Africa was a slow and piecemeal process so that some areas did not come under Roman control until the early third century AD. In 146 BC the Romans destroyed Carthage and occupied its territories as the province of Africa. The Romans subsequently annexed some Numidian territories following the Jugurthan War (111–105 BC), but it was not until 46 BC, when King Juba I chose the losing side in the Roman Civil War, that eastern Numidia became a Roman province. After this date Mauretania was ruled by the Roman client kings, Juba II and Ptolemy, until the Emperor Gaius had Ptolemy executed in AD 40 and the kingdom was converted into provinces (Map 2). These conquests did not mark the end of the process and from the reign of Vespasian (AD 69–79) onwards there was a gradual move south and west as more land was brought under direct Roman control. The movement of the *Legio III Augusta*, the principal unit of Roman Africa, demonstrates the direction of these conquests (see Map 3). The legion was stationed at Ammaedara before Vespasian's reign, when it was transferred south-west to Theveste, to be in closer proximity to the Aurès Mountains. Finally under Trajan (AD 98–117) it moved to Lambaesis to guard routes between the Aurès and the pre-desert regions beyond.

The chronology of conquest is important for the evolution of urbanism under the Romans. Acculturation between Romans and non-Romans in Africa was not a quick process and it took place at different speeds, at different times and with differential results from place to place. The influence of Roman culture permeated beyond its frontiers so that some cities, particularly in King Juba II's Mauretania, adopted elements of Roman-style urbanism before their incorporation into the Empire. To further complicate matters, as we have already seen, Africa was never a self-contained unit. Mediterranean contacts with Italy and the Greek East were important before

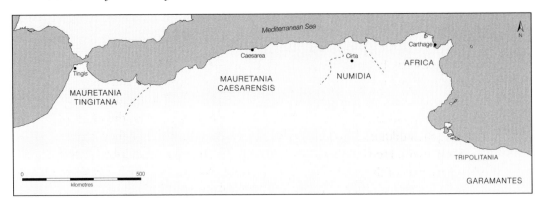

Map 2 Early Roman provinces.

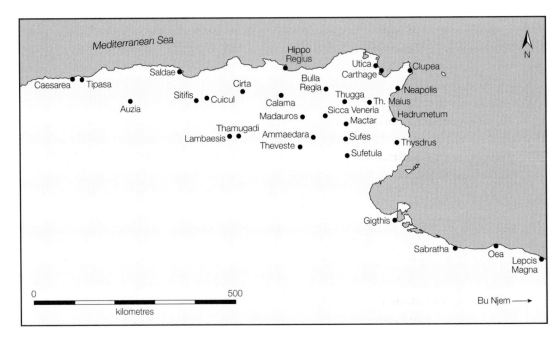

Map 3 Roman Africa Proconsularis, Numidia and Eastern Mauretania.

and during the Roman Empire. However, for many areas of Rome's African Empire it was only with conquest that the process of urbanisation began. The implantation of Roman colonies, populated by Roman settlers – either army veterans or people transplanted from Italy – further complicated the process by speeding up acculturation between Rome and some African cities. For other settlements there was a considerable time-lag between conquest and urbanisation. Time-lags are also evident between Africa and other areas of the Empire, so that we should not expect to see the same types of monuments being built in the same quantity in Africa as in Britain at exactly the same moment. Fashion and the diktats of local culture impacted upon how 'Romanisation' progressed and the form it took.

Romanisation?

It would be useful, before examining the ways in which African cities adopted Roman cultural forms, to look at what some of these were. 'Romanisation' and its features can be interpreted quite differently by academics. For instance, Broughton examined the organisation of the land and the legal definitions of the cities, barely considering the buildings and the ways of thought and customs that they represented (Broughton 1929). However, structures form the core of Roman urban living, the 'lived-experience' of the city's inhabitants. They supported the institutions, religion, economic activity and leisure pursuits of the population. It is important to note that not all of the elements discussed below needed to be present to make a city 'Roman'. Some cities did not build some of the structures discussed or built them late in their history. The buildings and activities that went on in them were part of a wider cultural vocabulary of what it was to be Roman (or Romano-African). The intensity of the desire to be seen as properly Roman, and what you needed to do to demonstrate that, changed over time.

The building types discussed here were common in Italian cities from the second century BC onwards and some had their origins at a rather earlier date in the Greek East. Monumental public architecture evolved over time and was still evolving in the late Roman Republican period and under the Empire, when African populations started to construct Roman-style buildings; African populations did not take on an established monumental set that was not subject to change. In Africa assessing 'Romanisation' is made more complicated because of the region's existing urban framework; as we have seen some African cultures had their own monumental building sets which overlapped with 'Roman' buildings; public squares, temples and city walls all pre-date the Roman conquest.

It is hard to pin down the extent to which the populations of Africa, and perhaps more particularly the economic and social elites of the cities, felt about Roman styles of urbanisation. Few literary texts give us much detail about how the writer interacted with and responded to their environment. For the most part we examine the way that populations adopted Roman building types, and the institutions and pastimes that these imply were taking place within them, but this is still complex. For instance, when a city erected an amphitheatre, a characteristically Roman cultural artefact, does this tell us that the population had ordered and paid for its construction because of its cultural intrinsic worth and therefore that pre-Roman populations were becoming Roman (Laurence et al. 2011)? Alternatively, was the city expressing loyalty to the state through its adoption of a key Roman cultural touchstone or was amphitheatre construction an expression of intra-elite and inter-city competition for popularity and status? Is the construction of the structure less to do with becoming Roman and more to do with being seen to be Roman for political advancement? Finally, does the rapid decline in amphitheatre construction after the second century AD tell us that the architectural type went in and out of fashion or that the games themselves were only periodically popular? In actuality, the construction of the amphitheatre as a place in which to hold spectacles and public punishments drew on all the elements mentioned above but, working from brief dedicatory building inscriptions and physical remains, it is difficult to be certain what the inhabitants of Thysdrus, for example, thought they were doing when they built three amphitheatres over a space of two centuries (Jouffroy 1986: 196, 232, 277).

The forum, often with a basilica where courts took place and the curia where the town council met, formed the heart of the Roman city. The city itself, if it were a new settlement, or if it was influenced by Punic or Greek ideas of urban planning, might be built on a street-grid, as was the case at pre-Roman Carthage. As in the pre-Roman period, temples were focal points for the city and the regions' cults but they were not the only place where the links between human and divine were expressed or sacred power was demonstrated. The theatre and amphitheatre were not just places where plays or spectacles took place; they also contained shrines and statues for the gods and were locations where religious ceremonies could take place. At the same time the festivals that took place within these structures and, for a few cities, chariot races in the circus were important leisure activities for the African population. Finally, a crucial element of Roman urban living was public bathing in purpose-built structures.

Republican Africa (146–31 BC)

The initial Roman occupation did not change cities markedly; there was no apparent desire to promote Roman-style urbanism in native towns. A governor was installed in Utica to control the new province of Africa but seven Punic cities, including Utica and Hadrumetum, which had abandoned Carthage during the war, technically became free allies of Rome and were rewarded with their own large territories (*lex agraria* 78–82). The process of rural organisation, the assigning of land to African cities, to Roman colonists and investors, started immediately with agricultural land being centuriated (assessed and regularly divided up) as a result of the tribune of the plebs, Gaius Gracchus', measures (122 BC) codified in the *lex agraria* (agrarian law) of 111 BC, which provided the base for future land organisation in the province (Broughton 1929: 20–5; Crawford 1996: 113–81). The occupied land became *ager publicus* (public land) and was largely farmed by indigenous populations either as *homines stipendiarii* (tributary communities) or were sold or leased to private individuals by the Roman state.

Africa was not subject to the introduction of large numbers of Roman colonies until after the Roman civil wars of the middle of the first century BC, when the victors needed land on which to settle their veterans. The most famous attempt to create a colony prior to Caesar occurred in 122 BC, when Gracchus attempted to have Carthage rebuilt as a Roman colony as part of his economic and social reforms at Rome, despite an interdict on building at the site after 146 BC (Plutarch, *C. Gracchus*, 10–11.2). The extent and consequences of the colonial foundation are much debated. Gracchus was murdered the following year but colonists had already been enrolled and received land to farm and rent out. Where the colonists lived is not clear; there

is no evidence that Carthage's remains were developed before the late first century
BC, when the site was remodelled and rebuilt as a colony, the *colonia Iulia Karthago*.
Plutarch believed that Carthage was still destroyed in 87 BC when he has Gaius
Marius, the victorious commander in the Jugurthan War, state that the city was in
ruins (Plutarch, *C. Marius*, 20; Appian, *Libyca*, 136). This may have been a clever rhe-
torical response to a dire political situation rather than a statement of fact, but the city
appears to have been founded again under Caesar or Augustus, with new colonists
perhaps bolstering the descendants of the Gracchan settlers.

Some settlements appear to have been created in the aftermath of the Jugurthan
War but the extent to which these can be considered new urban foundations is
unknown. Three cities, Uchi Maius, Thibaris and Thuburnica, apparently regarded
Marius as their founder but what this actually means in terms of urbanisation, much
less Romanisation, is unclear (*CIL* 8.26181, 15450, 15454–5; Bénabou 2005: 35–6). We
do know that there were Italian traders in Africa and Numidia before the outbreak of
the Jugurthan War; Sallust describes the massacre of foreigners by Jugurtha's followers
(Sallust, *B.Jug.* 25, 64). These traders had little 'Romanising' impact on Africa. Instead,
as we have already seen, local elites drew on native, Punic and Hellenistic/eastern
cultural elements in the pre-Roman period and this continued for some time after
the conquest. Indeed, it was Greek Hellenistic culture that was the pre-dominant
pan-Mediterranean culture of the period and many Italians would have been from
cities that were Greek in origin or cultural influence.

Carthage's destruction and Numidia's defeat in the Jugurthan War allowed
other cities to garner a greater share of Mediterranean trade and its resultant profits. Hadrumetum, Lepcis Magna and Sabratha all seem to have flourished after the
metropolis' fall; in Lepcis' case this is hardly surprising given that it allegedly paid a
tribute of one talent per day to Carthage before 146 BC (Livy, 34.62.3–5; Dore 1988:
74). Even if that was an exaggeration, or the tribute of the whole Tripolitanian region,
the city still lost a financial burden with the fall of Carthage. Within the Numidian
kingdom many more places are described as towns by the time of the Jugurthan
War than in previous eras (e.g. Suthul, Vaga, Thala and Capsa), although this might
be ascribed to our sources paying greater attention to the region. Ironically, most of
what we know about them for this period is that the Roman army destroyed them,
although they were later inhabited during the Roman period (Sallust, *B.Jug.* 12, 37,
47, 54–6, 92; Strabo 17.3.8, 12). Some cities destroyed in 146, for example Clupea
and Neapolis, were re-founded as colonies under Caesar; Clupea is also mentioned
in accounts of the Roman Civil War (*CIL*, 10.6104, 8.968; Caesar, *Civil War*, 2.23).
Roman destruction of a city rarely seems to have led to its total abandonment.

Perhaps the major beneficiary of Carthage's temporary obliteration was Utica. In
addition to benefiting from the removal of a major trade competitor, it was, until
the colony of Carthage was rebuilt, the Roman governor's residence, despite being
technically a free city, with the attendant benefits in status. It received substantial
additional territory as a reward for its actions in the Third Punic War and under
Octavian also received municipal rights (Appian, *Libyca*, 135; Sallust, *B.Jug.*, 64, 85;

Dio Cassius, *Roman History*, 49.16). Due to its importance, the city appears in our literary sources more frequently than many others and it was clearly a locus for specialist skills that could perhaps not be accessed elsewhere by the Romans. For instance, Marius is described as making a sacrifice and having a soothsayer inspect the remains at the city (Sallust, *B.Jug.*, 56). Elsewhere we learn that the city had a theatre by 49 BC and it was walled, almost certainly during the Punic period, with the *porta Bellica* (the gate of Baal?) and turret reinforcing being described in Caesar's works (Caesar, *Civil War*, 2.24; *African War*, 87–8). It may also have had an amphitheatre, a real sign of Romanisation, in the first century BC (Lézine 1968: 149). From the first century BC there was an area of orthogonal planning around a wide porticoed avenue in the city centre, which replaced earlier city organisation and may mean that the old coastal *forum/agora* was superseded by a large new square as part of the development. 'Temple A', which lies in this area of the city, dates from around 50 BC, but it was not built on the same alignment as the rest of the new development and its foundations seem to have utilised the remains of an earlier structure (Lézine 1968: 105–6). Such reuse might suggest that the remains of a preceding temple had been incorporated and that there was a need to preserve the sacral nature of the site. It is important to note that religious feeling could be more important than the aesthetic demands of a new planning dispensation; in the later Roman period there was continued attachment to temple sites even after communities had become Christian.

The Julio-Claudian & Flavian Period (31 BC–AD 98)

The wealth of African cities and the fecundity of their rural territories, which provided the bulk of their income, are evinced by the fines levied by Caesar on communities that had taken the Pompeian side during the Civil War. Thapsus and Hadrumetum, along with their corporations of foreign traders, were fined, Thysdrus was amerced by having to provide Caesar with a quantity of corn and Lepcis (probably Lepcis Magna) had to pay the huge annual sum of 3 million pounds of oil to Rome (*B.Afr.*, 98).

The fine levied on Lepcis, seemingly forgiven by the time of Augustus (31 BC–AD 14), did not substantially damage its fortunes. The late second century BC had seen the formal planning of large areas of the city south of the Old Forum area. From the very end of the first century BC through to the Flavian period members of the city elite financed a range of buildings that were immortalised through a series of inscriptions. Whether there was any sort of planned building programme is impossible to know. Members of the elite may have been influenced by the generosity of their peers; the need not to be outdone would have been a strong motivator given the competitive ethos of the classical elite. The works are varied, displaying almost the whole gamut of buildings associated with Roman culture. At the very least an amphitheatre, theatre, basilica, market, nine temples, honorific arches, a city wall and port buildings were all constructed by the end of the first century AD, whilst the *forum vetus* was paved

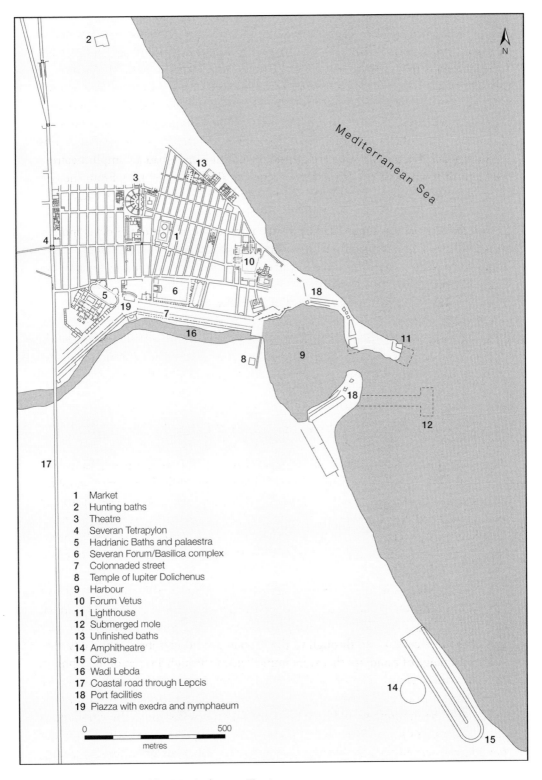

Fig. 2.1 Lepcis Magna: After Mattingly 1995: Fig. 6.1.

1   Market
2   Hunting baths
3   Theatre
4   Severan Tetrapylon
5   Hadrianic Baths and palaestra
6   Severan Forum/Basilica complex
7   Colonnaded street
8   Temple of Iupiter Dolichenus
9   Harbour
10 Forum Vetus
11 Lighthouse
12 Submerged mole
13 Unfinished baths
14 Amphitheatre
15 Circus
16 Wadi Lebda
17 Coastal road through Lepcis
18 Port facilities
19 Piazza with exedra and nymphaeum

0   500
metres

(see *AE* 1968: 549; *IRT*, 269, 273, 300, 306, 308, 321–4, 326–7, 330–3, 337–8, 340–2, 347–8 and 521). The work involved in these projects was immense. For instance the amphitheatre, sited some distance to the east of the city centre, seated around 16,000 people and was hollowed out of a hill with access provided by monumental passage-ways. The amphitheatre's cost was probably less than that of free-standing structures as the excavation of the hill meant that it could be supported by the landscape, but the man-hours involved in the construction was still impressive and cost implications went far beyond the actual building. There are maintenance costs for any structure: earthquake, fire, flood and time necessitate regular repairs and refurbishment, but putting on gladiatorial shows and beast hunts was extremely costly and was, at least in part, provided by individual members of the elite; in many communities the gift of games was a statutory requirement for those becoming city magistrates.

At Lepcis, Augustus' reign and that of his successor Tiberius (14–38 AD) saw an initial burst of activity, followed by a relative lull under the later Julio-Claudians (38–68 AD), before renewed construction under the Flavians (69-98 AD). This pattern could be ascribed to the city almost taking a financial breather after a long period of sustained investment in the city's aesthetics, its culture and in what was an overt expression of loyalty to Rome. It would be incorrect to see these fluctuations as the product of an 'African policy' by individual emperors as some have done (Aounallah 2001: 138). Although the Flavians, for instance, actively established the provincial imperial cult in Africa (see Chapter 3), for the most part change within cities was driven by local aristocracies.

Lepcis' early adherence to Roman-style monumental architecture is even more striking given that well into the imperial era the population still carried Punic names and neo-Punic (as the latest forms of the language are called) was being used in municipal inscriptions alongside Latin until the beginning of the second century, and in tomb contexts well into that century (Mattingly 1995: 119, 161; Fontana 2001; in both Plate 3 and Fig. 2.2 the neo-Punic appears under the Latin). Over time, however, Roman or Romanised names increasingly dominate at Lepcis, although the spoken language continued to exist in some areas of Africa for much longer. Augustine mentions the Punic language in the rural domains of his see of Hippo in the late fourth century (Millar 1968: 128–33; MacMullen 1966: 11–7; see also Chapter 6). Good examples of the continued use of Punic names alongside Roman ones at Lepcis are: Annobal Tapapius Rufus, son of Himilcho, who paid for the impressive new market in 9–8 BC, including a fountain and market benches and later paid for the theatre (*IRT*, 319, 321–3; Plates 6 and 7); and Iddibal Caphada Aemilius who paid for the *chalcidicum* (a place for storing bronze?), porticoes, gates and street paving (*IRT*, 324 b; Fontana 2001: 167). The presence of Punic in building inscriptions is paral-leled elsewhere in Africa until the second century AD; for instance at Volubilis' Temple B (Morestin 1980: 111; Jodin 1987: 220–1). In the first century Tripolitanian cities' coinage preserved Punic legends, particularly the city names (WY'T, SBRT'N and 'LPQY – transliterated into the Latin alphabet), alongside honorific Latin inscrip-tions to the emperors. As Fontana has shown in his study of the tombs of Lepcis in

Fig. 2.2 Forum Inscription *IRT*, 338.

the first two centuries AD, Latin was used for monumental inscriptions on the outside of tombs earlier than it was inside the tombs on cinerary urns, where Punic predominated into the second century (Fontana 2001: 166–8). The population of Lepcis was enthusiastic about the adoption of Latin monumental inscriptions and Roman-style buildings but their private lives were less open to cultural penetration and innovation than their public persona during the first century AD. It would be wrong to view this maintenance of earlier traditions as being an act, even subconsciously, of cultural resistance to the occupiers by non-elites. As Mattingly argues, there was no desire on the part of the Romans to turn the native populations into Romans but to get them to 'buy in' to aspects of Roman culture, which would make people much more likely to identify at least in part with the Empire, less likely to revolt and more likely to pay taxes (Mattingly 1995: 166). Such usage of both languages coupled with the large-scale building campaign at Lepcis and more modest work elsewhere shows that many populations were capable of dealing with the political realities of being under the control of a territorial empire whilst maintaining links to their ancient heritage. These two priorities were in no way incompatible. Dual identities, with different elements dominating in domestic and public settings, are a reasoned response to varied demands on cultural, political and religious affiliation (Adams 2004: 207–8, 213).

Lepcis is a relatively rare example of a city commemorating the construction of buildings with monumental inscriptions before the end of the first century AD. Only Carthage, Hippo Regius and Utica demonstrate documented building work in the century before the birth of Christ and fewer monuments still can be definitively dated before the more significant date, in this context, of 31 BC and Octavian/Augustus becoming sole ruler of the Roman world (*CIL*, 1.788, 10.6104, Pliny, *H.N.*, 5.24, 29). It is notable that all of these cities were ports and were therefore more likely to be receptive to external influences than inland cities and, as we have already seen, Utica, the rebuilt Carthage and Lepcis all had close ties to Rome.

Relatively few cities, including most of the colonies established under Caesar and Augustus, such as Curubis, Maxula and Uthina, are recorded as undertaking building work during the first century AD. However, the situation changed slowly during the course of that century and the populations of cities such as Thugga, Mactar, Sabratha and even Zithia, which shows little other evidence for construction throughout the Roman period, started to construct multiple monuments and record that they had done so. Far more common before the second century AD is the situation displayed in cities such as Thinissut or Uchi Maius, which record only one temple being built during the period. Overall across the region 24 out of the 32 cities that display evidence for building works before the second century AD built at least one temple and 53 out of the 118 buildings (45 per cent) demonstrated through archaeological remains, inscriptions and texts were temples (Jouffroy 1986: 175–200; *AE*). These building patterns suggest that the key relationship for many populations of the first century AD was between humans and the gods, and that being able to take part in Roman-style bathing and entertainment was relatively unimportant (see Chapter 3 for more on traditional religion). Of course we do not have evidence of all the building that went on in the period. Populations might think it unnecessary to put up an inscription recording the establishment of the building, whilst much evidence has been destroyed or awaits discovery, but it seems unlikely that temple inscriptions would have been disproportionately preserved compared to other structures.

Away from the coast and the heavily urbanised zones of Africa Proconsularis, there is very little evidence of building work taking place. Mauretania, independent until AD 40, is particularly under-represented in the epigraphy and archaeology, with only the old Punic coastal cities of Tipasa and Iol, renamed as Caesarea in Augustus' honour, demonstrating their urban quality in the same way as towns to the east (Fig. 2.3). Additionally, under Augustus, around 27–25 BC, nine colonies were placed into the region to boost Rome's strategic hold over the area, to support Juba II and Ptolemy, and to settle civil war veterans (Bénabou 1976: 55–6); other pre-existing cities had their status raised in the course of the first century. As Mauretania's capital and the chief residence of its kings, first-century Caesarea received a theatre, several temples, a huge wall circuit, probably an amphitheatre and forum, harbour installations, royal

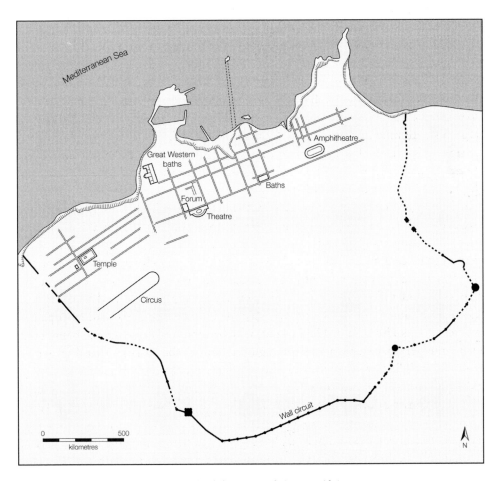

Fig. 2.3 Caesarea: after Gsell, S. 1952. *Cherchel, Antique Iol-Caesarea*, Algiers.

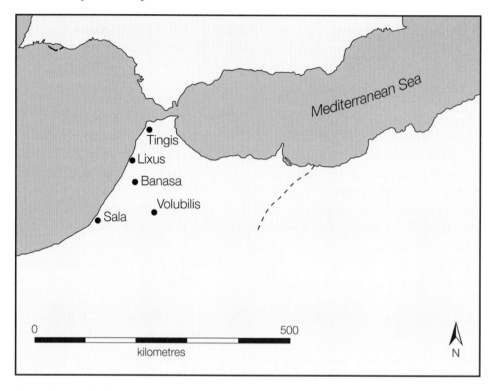

Map 4 Mauretania Tingitana.

palace and baths; the date of the circus is much less certain (Duval 1946; Picard 1976; Golvin & Leveau 1979: 841–2; Leveau 1984: 29–54; Roller 2003: 121–7, 153; Humphrey 1986: 310 n.17). Given the particularity of circumstances at Caesarea we should not be surprised that it does not conform to the building patterns of other first-century cities. Juba had been raised in the households of Julius Caesar and Augustus and he clearly wanted his capital to compete with, and echo, the glory not only of Rome, which was experiencing unprecedented monumentalisation under Augustus, but also the great eastern cities such as Alexandria and the capitals of eastern client-kings, such as Herod the Great, who were also conducting huge building campaigns. The expenditure involved in providing these facilities was immense and resources from the entire kingdom must have been employed. The types of buildings constructed demonstrate the elements of Mediterranean culture that Juba wanted to bring to his kingdom and pre-empt the priorities of Roman colonists and native elites throughout Africa over the next several hundred years. The structures provided space for leisure, religion, governance and social interaction, but how the populace actually related to the structures and the ways in which they were employed is more difficult to reconstruct. In the case of the early forum this is even more problematic because it has not been discovered. Its existence is hypothesised on the basis of the ubiquity of a forum in a Romanised city and the presence of Augustan era architectural elements in the forum of the third century;

the Juban forum may have been utterly cleared away during later building works and elements re-employed (Potter 1995: 35). Juba's efforts were certainly impressive and after his son's execution, Claudius raised the city to the status of colony, without the imposition of any colonists (Pliny *H.N.*, 5.1).

A clutch of building programmes documented at Tingitanan cities are an interesting counterpoint to the huge gaps in the epigraphic and archaeological record in Caesarensis (Map 4). The dating for many of these structures is not terribly precise and relies on the style of the structures rather than numismatic or epigraphic evidence, but it seems that building was occurring during Juba's reign and continued after Mauretanian integration into the Empire in the mid-first century AD. Colonies of veterans appear to have been established in Mauretanian territory at Banasa, Zulil and Babba in Tingitana early in Augustus' reign, while Lixus and Tingis were raised to the rank of colony and Volubilis to a *municipium* under Claudius. It may be that Juba's pro-Roman attitude and the influence of Roman colonists led to a wave of construction at the cities (Pliny, *H.N.*, 5.2–5, 20–1; Strabo 3.1.8; Roller 2003: 96–7). Banasa, Lixus, Thamusida, Sala and Volubilis built temples; Thamusida and Volubilis built bath houses; and around the mid-first century AD Volubilis and Sala both laid out *fora*, accompanied in Sala's case with a capitol, the quintessentially Roman temple to Jupiter Capitolinus, Juno and Minerva (Ponisch 1982: 831–3, 840–3; Morestin 1980; Jouffroy 1986: 181, 185, 196). Perhaps the most intriguing structure is Lixus' amphitheatre, given that it was in a territory outside of direct Roman control and what we have said about the intensely Roman nature of the amphitheatre and its games (Ponisch 1982: 842; Sear 2006: 271). After all, at this date there may only have been one other stone-built amphitheatre in Africa, at Utica, but the impact of Roman colonies in the region and Juba's pro-Roman attitude combined to produce a flowering Roman influenced culture on the edge of the Mediterranean world.

Turning to the Roman colonists, we should not necessarily think of the veterans as farming the land they were granted themselves; given that most would have had little knowledge of agriculture after 25 years in the Roman army such a situation would probably have ended in disaster (Cherry 1998: 147). Instead they owned the land and pre-existing native populations would have continued to farm with much of the profit from produce sold in African cities or exported abroad going to the colonists (see Plate 8 for olive oil production facilities at Thuburbo Maius). This use of native agrarian populations for the benefit of the colonists but also members of local or Roman elites, senators who were large landowners (Pliny claimed that six senators owned most of Africa during Nero's reign; Pliny, *H.N.*, 18.35) and the emperors, forms the centre of debates over the role of Rome in Africa. Certainly the exploitative nature of the relationship saw more benefits of Roman rule accruing to elites than to the poor (Shaw 1983: 140). To some extent Roman rule only continued earlier patterns: Carthaginian or royal Numidian landowners, themselves exploiters of the peasantry were replaced by absentee landlords based at Rome or new city elites, but this should not permit us to be blind to the abusive nature of the relationship or to the fact that considerable African wealth was diverted to Rome and to the African

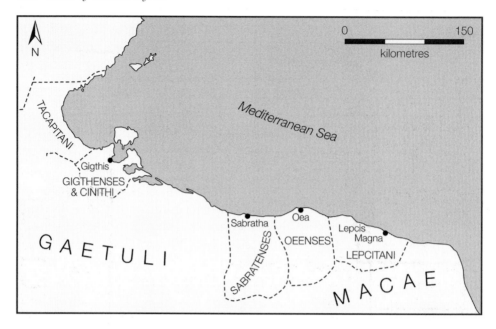

Fig. 2.4 Lepcitanian territory: after Mattingly 1995: Fig. 4.3.

cities. It was on the backs of the rural poor that the elite were able to furnish lavish private houses and create monumental cityscapes; the stunning remains of the cities would not have existed without the elite's ability to exploit their domains' agricultural potential.

The African city was not just the urban area. All towns had a rural territory that belonged to and was governed from it, and which varied greatly in size. Some, for instance Carthage, Lepcis Magna and Cirta, had immense areas under their control, whilst in the Bagradas valley in Proconsularis or on Cap Bon, because of the high density of cities, territories were correspondingly small, which makes their monumentality even more impressive and demonstrates the fecundity of their lands (Broughton 1929: 70–6; Mattingly 1995: 140–1; Duncan-Jones 1963: 85–90; Fig. 2.4). Unlike other areas of the Empire (including Mauretania Caesarensis) this produced intensive, small-scale urbanisation. This dense urbanism may have driven construction. With the neighbouring city being so close it would be easy to see their urban development on a regular basis and seek to better it.

The town and its hinterland was one and the same political institution and many urban inhabitants would have owned or even worked its land. Towns could be distribution centres into which imports from outside the region were brought or agricultural exports could be gathered prior to movement to the coast. They were also centres for commerce, where people who lived in the countryside would have been able to purchase goods that were not produced on the estates where they lived. As we have already seen at Lepcis, shops were a key feature of the urban architecture, with purpose-built structures lining main roads and being integral parts of some *fora* (see Fig. 2.5 for shops at Thamugadi's forum). Market days provided an opportunity

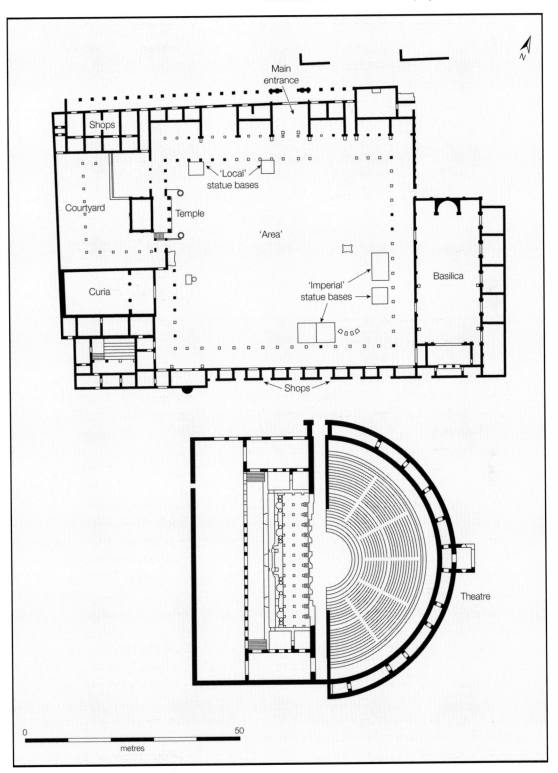

Fig. 2.5 Thamugadi's forum: after Ballu 1897: Plate 12.

for urban and rural populations to come together as well as an occasion on which town or provincial magistrates could demonstrate their power and munificence.

For Sitifis a colony of Roman veterans, the *Colonia Nerviana Augusta Martialis Veteranorum Sitifensium*, founded in Mauretania Caesarensis in the reign of Nerva (AD 96–98), Fentress has argued that its economy was separate from that of the imperially owned estates surrounding it. She argues that the agricultural produce of these estates worked by tenant farmers (*coloni*), and the subsequent profits, flowed out of the region to the coast and then Rome without entering the city (apart from rather meagre sums that the workers were able to make by selling surpluses they harvested above and beyond their subsistence needs and the share of the crop they were bound to give to the imperial estate – Fentress 1990: 119–21; Sears 2007: 64). While it may be true that imperial estates did not benefit local cities as much as if the lands had been owned by local aristocrats, who could plough their profits into the local economy rather than Rome, it did give the Roman state a continuing interest in ensuring that African estates remained productive and peaceful. The occasional construction of monuments under the auspices of provincial governors may reflect a need to return wealth from the imperial system back to the region to keep the locals happy.

Alongside market days, city and country were also bound together by religious festivals, which incorporated processions and games in the theatre and amphitheatre. These occasions would have brought the community together in worship and/or entertainment, but also would have emphasised the importance of the elite who sat in the prime locations in the theatre, in a section often divided off from the rest of the population by barriers with special seats for the magistrates, and as priests presided over worship and were at the head of religious processions. The social hierarchy was hardwired into all aspects of African society. As was discussed above, the inhabitants created their built environment which then served to inculcate the values expressed in its structure to generation after generation of citizens (Giddens 1984; Laurence et al. 2011). Buildings were not just there to host entertainment or religious worship but to educate the population on how society worked and their place within it.

City Government & Elite Competition

The exact number of colonies placed into Africa Proconsularis between Caesar taking control of the Roman world and the end of the first century AD is difficult to ascertain. Any list is based on an incomplete epigraphic record and Pliny the Elder's *Natural History*, which contradict each other on occasion because of changes over time, but as many as nine colonies were placed into Africa, for instance, under Augustus (Pliny, *H.N.*, 5.24–9). Further colonies were created during the first century AD. For example, Ammaedara was turned into a colony under the Flavians (AD 69–96) when the legion departed (*CIL*, 8.308). Presumably the city already had army veterans living there before the upgrade in status, the product of decades of retirement

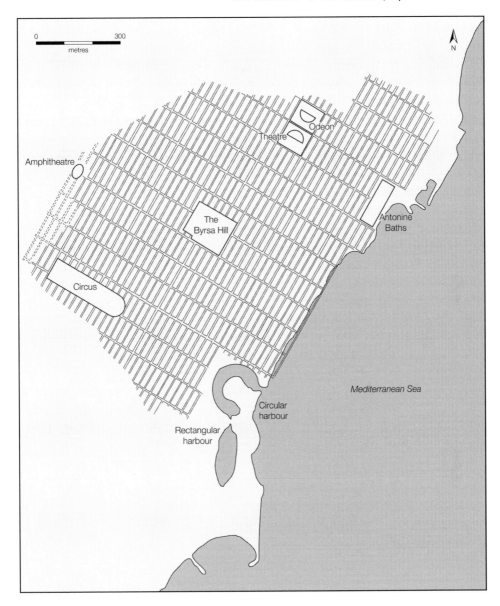

Fig. 2.6 Roman Carthage: after Ennabli 1997: 6.

from the army. The regularisation of the town would have left a body of Roman citizens at a strategic site as the army pushed south-westwards.

Taking Carthage as a case study, not all of its colonists were based in the city itself. Communities of colonists (*pagi*) were located throughout the city's territory at native settlements such as Thugga or Thuburbo Maius (e.g. *AE* 1905: 19; *CIL*, 8.848; Rives 1995: 104–5). Some of the native settlements are called *civitates* and some *castella* by our sources, with the latter being less urban and more like strongholds of local populations; Thugga and Thuburbo Maius were *civitates*. A similar process may have happened with the colony of Uthina, which had sites such as the *pagus Mercurialis* nearby (Maurin 1995: 97–135). These arrangement led to dual community situations where the non-Roman community's (the *civitas*') governmental structure was recognised alongside the colonists, leading to both communities contributing to the construction of the monumental urban topography, sometimes to the same monument. For instance, at Thugga, an altar to the Divine Augustus and to Claudius, from the reign of Claudius (AD 41–54), was paid for by a member of the native community who was given the insignia of a *sufete* (a chief magistrate in Punic cities) in thanks, but the altar was dedicated by the patron of the *pagus* (*CIL*, 8.26517). Here a native paid for the monument and the leading figure in the politically dominant Roman community dedicated it. Public ritual and inscription announced the domination; over time that relationship would become more of a partnership. Although at cities such as Thugga there was a dual organisation, this does not mean that there was a dual site with native and colonist occupying physically separate spaces. Poinssot, one of the excavators of Thugga, believed such separation existed but, as Saint-Amans has rightly pointed out, this view was conditioned by twentieth-century societal realities, where French colonist and Arab peasant were physically separated in new and old towns, rather than by archaeological evidence (Saint-Amans 2004: 59–60; Khanoussi 1992: 597–602; Rives 1995: 119 repeats the old view). The *pagi* initially did not have their own magistrates as they were administered from Carthage, but over time this changed as the colonists gained more autonomy (Rives 2007: 104–5). There would have been status differentials between the two communities because Roman citizenship brought additional legal rights, including economic benefits and exemption from torture, but over time intermarriage between the groups and the granting of citizenship to prominent Africans would have served to diminish the differences between the communities. The differences between colonist and provincial disappeared across the Empire in the early third century when Caracalla's *Constitutio Antoniniana* abolished the distinction.

The colonies had a political organisation that reflected that of Rome itself. The inscription that is generally used to enlighten the rule and organisation of these communities comes from Urso in Spain (the *Lex Coloniae Genetivae*), but many clauses within the text must be indicative of the structure of other colonies as the officers mentioned in the text are present across the Roman world (see Crawford 1996: 393–454). Colonies were governed on a day-to-day basis by a panel of four magistrates, two *duumviri* and two *aediles*, who were elected annually. There was also a permanent town council, comprised of the decurions (*ordo decurionum*), the town councillors, who acted as an advisory and decision making body and provided the permanent political stability within the town. Additionally, municipal priests – pontiffs and augurs (three of each in the case of Urso) – were appointed (*Lex Coloniae Genetivae*, 66–8). Finally, every five years the *duumviri* were designated as *duumviri quinquennales* and undertook a census with the power to adlect (bring in) new members into the *ordo*. All of these titles can be seen on public inscriptions from Africa during the Roman Empire.

Some Punic cities and native *civitates* and *castella* improved their status from tributary communities throughout the first two centuries AD. Important cities like Utica under Octavian, but also more minor ones such as Thubursicum Numidarum under Trajan (AD 98–117 – *ILAlg.*, 1.1240), became *municipia*, which made their inhabitants Roman citizens who could maintain their own laws and magistrates if they wanted to do so, although many did not. Eventually some cities were also accorded the rank of colony without having colonists implanted into the city; effectively native elites were co-opted into the Roman system.

In the first and early second century AD many pre-Roman communities kept the Punic name *sufete* for their magistrates; at Abbir in Proconsularis the practice continued into the 180s (*CIL*, 8.26517; *AE*, 1982: 932). Another example comes from between Capsa and Aquae Tacapitanae in the south of Proconsularis. There a dedication to Trajan by two *sufetes*, Atticus and Fronto Masla, demonstrates this continuity with the past whilst at the same time honouring the emperor (*CIL*, 8.22796):

AVG SACRVM

PRO SAL(UTE) IMP NERVAE (TRAIANI) CAES AVG GER DACIC

... SVFETIBVS ATTICO ET FRONTONE MASLAE

Consecrated to Augustus

For the salutation of the Emperor Nerva Trajan Caesar Augustus vanquisher of the Germans and Dacians

... the sufetes Atticus and Fronto Masla

Even Lepcis continued to appoint *sufetes* until AD 107, when it became a colony and adopted Roman offices. Punic titles or ideas also probably lurk behind Latin phrases, such as *ornator patriae* (adorner of the fatherland) or *praefectus sacrorum* (prefect of sacred matters), not found in Roman colonies (Fontana 2001; e.g. *IRT*, 321). As with much else in the Roman Empire, particularity rules and individual cities may have used the title *sufete* in slightly different ways (Aounallah 2001: 191). All of these cases demonstrate Rome's lack of interest in imposing their own administrative systems on to pre-existing cities.

City magistrates were important for the built environment as they not only controlled building within the city and prevented damage to public buildings and roads, but they were also required, as a condition of becoming magistrate, to pay a *summa honoraria* (an honorary sum) for the provision of building or games (*munera*) (Duncan-Jones 1974: 67–8). Voluntary *ob honorem* (through honour) payments could be made by officials who really wished to emphasise their wealth. The level of the *summa honoraria* varied considerably from city to city, with city size and status being reflected in the price an individual had to pay (Duncan-Jones 1974: 67–8). So, for instance, at the end of the first century a man paid for the construction of the 'Flavian' temple at Lepcis Magna probably when he became a *sufete* (although the inscription is damaged, only '*re sufeta*' survives – *IRT*, 348). The cost of the temple – 80,000 sesterces – is far beyond the cost of any *summa honoraria* in Africa and must therefore reflect an additional gift.

Individuals paid to hold magistracies because of the status they conferred on the individual and the family. In paying for the offices individuals demonstrated their wealth to the rest of society, potentially bringing themselves and their families to the attention of the wider world, including provincial governors. Finally, there was also a desire to showcase the individual's love of their hometown by ornamenting it with the key elements of Roman-African civilisation discussed in this chapter.

The provision of statues and buildings by magistrates was only one element of the compulsory payment. There are frequent references in the inscriptions to payments to the populace in the form of *sportulae* (gifts), spectacles or *epulum* (a banquet). For instance, from Giufi comes an altar of blue limestone that was dedicated:

> To the Genius of the most splendid order of the decurions of the town of *Alexandriani Giufitani* by Publius Pompeius Geminius, son of Publius, of the tribe Papiria, and Gaius Areius Rogatus son of Rogatus, of the tribe Papiria, former quaestors and aediles who through their own generosity made the dedication of the altar and out of dedication gave a banquet to the decurions. The location was given by decree of the decurions. [*AE* 2003: 1985]

These individuals were not paying for magistracies but were making a euergetistic gift to the city. The key audience for the act of generosity were the decurions who were given the banquet; their peers were those who mattered in the eyes of the former magistrates. In Africa, as elsewhere in the Empire, the desire to emphasise one's generosity produced the tendency to publicise the amount that had been spent on a monument or games in order that your contribution to the city could be set against that of other members of the elite. So at Lepcis, in AD 72, Iddibal Balsillecis, son of Annobal, grandson of Asmun, ornamented and built the Temple of Magna Mater with 200,000 sesterces of his own money (*IRT*, 300). Here Iddibal and his family were maintaining their identity through their use of non-Roman names whilst also commemorating their generosity in a thoroughly Roman way: in a Latin inscription.

The *summa honoraria* and *ob honorem* gifts helped to link magistrates to their home town and inscribed their relationship on to the city; their generosity could be read and re-read over centuries. This provided an ongoing status for their descendants and educated future generations as to how a magistrate should behave. This gave an element of continuity to the town and the populace as well as examples to be imitated and surpassed in the future. The drivers for the production of an urban landscape also provide context to when and where 'Roman' buildings were constructed in Africa during the first century AD.

Rome in Africa?

The early imperial period marks a significant evolution in Africa's relationship with Rome. Imperial policy led to the introduction of colonies under Caesar and

Augustus and the rewarding of superior statuses to other communities such as Utica or Ammaedara. There was clearly a desire for Rome's commendation in that way: all evidence from the Empire suggests that cities lobbied for these honours as a way of demonstrating their city's status within their region (Aulus Gellius, 16.13; Aounallah 2001: 175). Some local elites began to express their social and urban identities through the medium of 'Roman' monumental construction or dedicatory inscriptions, but this movement, when compared with contemporary urban populations in Italy, was limited (Jouffroy 1986).

The adoption of Roman-style nomenclature, buildings and religion can be seen as an ad hoc and gradual process with old magistracies being retained in some places and not in others. Some magistrates clearly retained native names whilst others adopted Roman names, 'Romanised' their own names or took on new Roman names. It is unclear what these individuals thought taking a new name or putting up a Latin inscription actually meant in terms of their identity. Presumably Annobal Tapapius Rufus, son of Himilcho, believed his Lepcitanian citizenship was deeply important and could ground that in a wider Punic culture. However, he was also an inhabitant of the Roman Empire and his father clearly felt it important to give him some Roman sounding names, though whether that was because of loyalty to Rome, a desire for political advancement or fashion is unknowable. The fact that *sufetes*, Punic funerary inscriptions and traditional names were all in use should not, however, be seen as a conscious snub to Rome. It, like the adoption of some 'Romanised' elements, was a complex negotiation of ideas that preserved the cultural heritage of the city and perhaps more importantly the family, whilst at the same time adapting to the new political and cultural realities of the Roman Empire. Throughout the first century AD the populations of Africa undertook such adaptation to benefit themselves in their own competitions for glory and recognition.

3

Traditional Religious Life

Variety

Given the centrality of religious expression to ancient populations, it is important to consider the effect of the Roman occupation on African urban religion. Just as Africa does not demonstrate uniformity in terms of Roman occupation and urbanisation, we should not expect to see universal conformity in religious beliefs and practices; individual populaces adhered to their own sets of cults that resembled those pantheons worshipped in other cities but were not identical. This chapter will examine this diversity by examining how different cities and communities reacted to the penetration of Punic and Roman cultures and their different ways of expressing the relationship between man and god. It will also examine local cults that maintained 'native' features throughout the Roman period. This variety should neither, necessarily, be regarded as resistance to Roman culture nor a weakness in Rome's ability to impose their culture on others. The Romans did not usually see it as necessary to impose a religious structure on native populations. Indeed, the only religious practice that the Romans banned in Africa was human sacrifice (Tertullian, *Apology*, 9). Instead these cults will be viewed through the understanding that the adoption of 'Romanised' cults by native populations was the product of contact between Roman officials and settlers and native populations, as well as African elites' visits to Rome and other Italian cities. The incorporation of Roman ideas and practices was the product of local people's decisions about how to use those religious conceptions for their own benefit.

The *Interpretatio Romana* & Religious Continuity

The representation of some gods gradually changed in the Roman period. From the first century AD onwards many communities shifted from expressing their chief deities in traditional terms to a semi-'Romanised' conception of the gods that persisted to the end of Africa; this is the process of syncretism described by Tacitus as the *Interpretatio Romana* (Tacitus, *Germania*, 43.3). However it is often difficult to approach what exactly lay behind the Romanised gloss of a deity and such veneers should not be seen as applied with any sort of rule across Africa. A good example of these processes can be seen with the chief Carthaginian deities Tanit and Baal, who gradually became equated (usually) with the Roman deities Caelestis and Saturn (Rives 1995: 162–5). So while the Sabrathan open-air sanctuary was dedicated to Baal and Tanit, a dedication to the Roman goddess Caelestis has also been found in its vicinity (Brouquier-Reddé 1992: 27–9; Longerstay 1995: 843; *IRT*, 2). This process of assimilation took a long time and the cult of Baal Hammon, rather than that of Saturn, appeared or intensified in some places during the first century AD and it is also noticeable that the African Caelestis and Saturn were very different to the understanding of those deities in other regions, such as Italy (Cadotte 2007: 25–9, 68–81).

Evidence of the lack of homogeneity in African religion can be seen in the fact that in some regions, and especially at military settlements that brought in personnel from beyond Africa, Saturn was often paired with Ops, a Roman fertility deity, rather than Caelestis (Le Glay 1966: II.82). At Hadrumetum no equivalence between Baal Hammon and Saturn seems to have been made; instead Pluto was the vehicle for the populace to express the religious ideas surrounding their chief deity (Cadotte 2007: 27, 333–4, 366). Subsequently, when Hadrumetum became a colony under Trajan it took the name *Colonia Concordia Ulpia Traiana Augusta Frugifera Hadrumetina*, the Frugifera element expressing the fertility aspect of the deity (*CIL*, 6.1687). Hadrumetum's ambiguity in how the god's name was expressed is not unique. Neptune, who had a distribution throughout Africa from Lepcis Magna, where a temple was built during the first century AD (*IRT*, 306), all the way west to Saldae in Mauretania, is a case in point. In the area of Africa that became Byzacena, Cadotte has argued that the name Neptune was given to a pre-Roman Libyan fertility deity (Cadotte 2007: 314–9). In other areas of Africa, as elsewhere in the Empire, Neptune was the name for a plethora of local deities of springs or for gods of the sea (Rives 1995: 130–1; Cadotte 2007: 319–23). The former is demonstrated by the number of times a cult place is located close to a water source, for instance at Zaghouan (Plate 11), the source of the second-century aqueduct that provided water to Carthage, or at the hillside spring of Aïn Drinn above Lambaesis, which in the mid-second century AD also functioned as a site where the slaves of the legates of the legion honoured their masters (Marcillet-Jaubert 1970: 213–20). These differences indicate the willingness on the part of local populations to adopt Roman names and to use them in different ways in order to convey aspects of their protective deities to wider populations whilst at core maintaining ancient beliefs.

Just as Punic deities continued to be worshipped well into the Roman period, albeit usually under Roman names, non-Punic gods also occur in Roman Africa into the fourth century and beyond. Some are known in groups or pantheons of deities but others are known as singular divinities. The preservation of the names of these local divinities mark not so much resistance to Roman power behind the names of ancient gods, but ways of accommodating local heritage with a new political reality and often using Roman media – statues, temples and inscriptions. Although the construction of a temple to a native god at a city was a relatively rare phenomenon in Africa, during Septimius Severus' reign (193–211) at Magifa the gods Masidenis, Thililuae, Sugganis, Iesdanis and Masiddice had a temple containing their statues built for them (*ILAlg.*, 1.2977). Not all native deities were expressed through purely Romanised media. A group of native and Punic gods are known from a pictorial stele found near Vaga accompanied by an inscription to the gods Macurtam, Macurgum, Vihinam, Bonchor, Varsissima, Matilam and Iunam by M. Aemilius Ianuarius and Q. Aelius Felix (Camps 1954: 234–5; Picard 1954: 24; *AE* 1948: 114). The images of the gods are the product of local artistic traditions; it is not a Roman figured relief in any way and that in itself could be seen as a rejection of (or perhaps inability to produce) Roman art forms. The inscription, however, is in Latin and the dedicators, whatever their ethnic origins, bear Roman names.

Pre-Roman deities remained important into the sixth century, at least on the periphery of Roman Africa. Corippus' account of the campaigns of John Troglita against the Libyan tribes characterises them as pagans worshipping deities, including the bull-headed Gurzil in contrast to the Christian populations of Roman Africa (Corippus, *Iohannidos*, 8.300–20). Whether such a centre/periphery opposition reflects reality is hard to say; it may well just mean that Corippus did not, or did not want to, believe that real Roman citizens could be pagan rather than that none were. Corippus' dichotomy of Christian Africa and pagan tribe does though parallel the earlier Roman situation, albeit some native gods were worshipped in Roman cities. For instance, as Mattingly points out for Tripolitania, there was a deep divide between the deities worshipped in the cities: Punic deities clothed in Roman names with an element of more exotic eastern cults; and the interior: native Libyan deities such as Mars Canapphar (albeit he had been syncretised with a Roman god) (Mattingly 1995: 168).

Regionality

Local preference for individual or groups of deities is a 'constant' throughout the region. To take Caelestis and Saturn as an example, the divine couple appear to have had few temples or stelae dedicated to them in Tripolitania or western Mauretania (Le Glay 1966: 266–7). Apart from the Sabrathan sanctuary, another at Gheran, a rural sanctuary in Lepcitanian territory at Ras el-Mergheb and dedications from Sabratha, Zitha and Medina Doge (*Mesphe*), they are strikingly absent from the region;

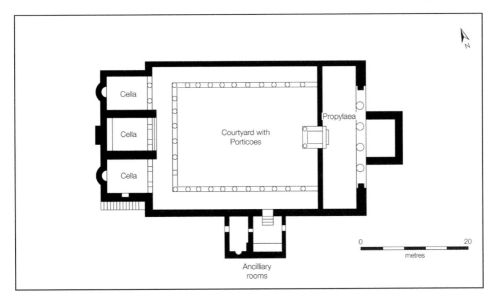

Fig. 3.1 Temple of Saturn at Thugga: after Le Glay 1961: Fig. 4.

suggestions of the existence of temples at Sabratha is without any real evidence (Broquier-Reddé 1992: 29–30, 48–55, 125–6; Mattingly 1995: 127, 133, 168; *IRT*, 268; Bénabou 1976: 261–80). The emporia's Punic populations then, although influenced and dominated by Carthage in the pre-Roman period, continued to prefer their own patron deities Liber Pater and Hercules, Roman expressions of Shadrapa and Milk'Ashtart (see Chapter 2). Lepcis had temples to Liber Pater and Milk'Ashtart on the *forum vetus* from the very early first century AD. Di Vita argues that Milk'Ashtart's original temple was taken over by a cult to Rome and Augustus in the late first century BC, with the Punic deity being moved to a smaller temple in the forum's northern corner; however the actual evidence for such a process of marginalisation is limited (Di Vita 1982: 553–8; Cadotte 2007: 253–66, 283–305).

Elsewhere in first century Africa fertility deities such as Saturn/Baal, the Cereres, Tellus and Frugifer had more temples built to them than any other group of deities, reflecting the crucial importance of agriculture to life across the ancient world. Of course these deities can demonstrate or mask different religious traditions with, for example, Tellus being an Italian chthonian goddess and Saturn having Punic roots. Settlements of all sizes and civic statuses across Proconsularis built temples to fertility deities: Carthage had a temple to Tellus by 40 BC; Vaga had one by 2 BC; Thugga, Bir Derbal, Uchi Maius and Henchir el-Hammam built temples of Saturn in the first century AD; while Hippo Regius had a sanctuary of Baal-Saturn and Thinissut a sanctuary of Baal and Tanit during the first century AD (*CIL*, 10.6104, 8.14392 and 8.26241, *ILAfr.*, 558; Le Glay 1961: 287–9, 431ff; and 1966: 11; Cadotte 2007: 68–9). The Thinissut sanctuary was a complex structure with multiple shrines, courtyards, stelae and a range of statuary, including the famous terracotta statue of the goddess depicted as a draped woman with a lion's head (leontocephalous), as well as fully

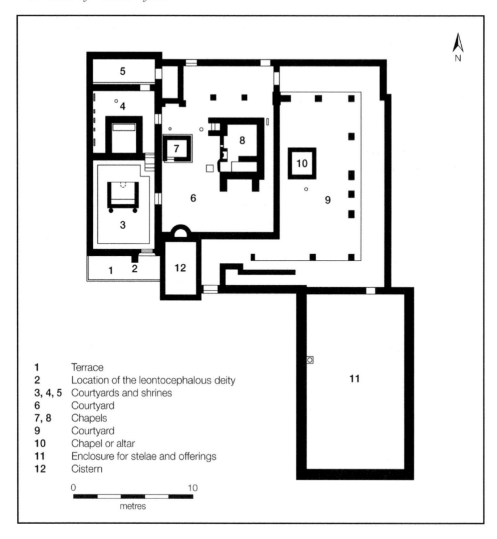

Fig. 3.2 Temple of Thinissut: after Le Glay 1961: Fig. 2.

anthropomorphic statues of the deity. A neo-Punic inscription, 'to Lord Baal and to Tanit the face of Baal the two sanctuaries', and Latin dedications to Saturn and two others to a deity starting with the letter C (Caelestis?) not only confirm the links between the Punic and Romanised deities but are also notable for the changes in the way that devotees progressed from describing the deity in Punic to Latin (*KAI*, 137, *ILAfr.*, 307–10; Cadotte 2007: 69–70; Aounallah 2001: 309–15). The syncretic links between the deities demonstrate the local population's desire to accommodate Roman ways of expressing religious belief whilst maintaining their heritage; the iconography at Thinissut demonstrates links back to the Punic period and, in the leontocephalic statues, connections to the animal-headed deities of Egypt. African cults therefore show cultural dialogues between Rome and Africa, but also across the Mediterranean more generally. However, new artistic, technical and linguistic elements in the 'Romanised' cults would have impacted on the way that devotees responded to and understood the deities.

The Temples

What is a temple? At some level this seems to be an unnecessary question. A temple is after all a place where a deity was worshipped by a community or part of a community but in Africa sacred places at urban locations varied greatly. We have already seen different types of religious sites in the pre-Roman period. Both open-air areas containing dedications and sacrifices, often without substantial buildings, and more formal temples were used in Africa. In the Roman period both of these traditions continued, although temple buildings come to predominate, a fashion that was clearly influenced at least in part by what Romans thought was the proper way to treat the gods, but perhaps also because increasing elaboration in temple architecture could be used by elites to advertise their own worth. That is not to say that the Roman period saw a great break with what had gone before. The changes in cultic 'furniture' took place over three centuries or more and at different rates in different cities. Again, local particularities predominate even if those local traditions would be intelligible to other African communities. A visitor walking through the cities of the region would see many similarities in building types, city layout and religious experience, but there would always be differences from place to place because of the range of cultural influences at work – 'native', Punic, Hellenistic and Roman.

Taking Hadrumetum as an example, the *tophet* there was in use into the second century AD but the final phase was very different in structure and contents than in the pre-Roman phases (Le Glay 1961: 255). Funerary urns containing human remains were replaced with small perfume jars, suggesting that libations (liquid offerings) to the god had become the core of the ritual rather than the dedication of the dead (Cintas 1947: 77–80). Other sites also show change coupled with continuity. Thugga's sanctuary of Baal Hammon continued in use but was gradually monumentalised after the first century (Saint-Amans 2004: 348–59; Le Glay 1961: 207–20). Across the Gulf of Tunis from Carthage the sanctuary of *Saturnus Balcaranensis* (from the Punic Baal Qarnaïm, Lord of the Two Horns) on the Djebel Bou Kourneïn (the Mountain of the Two Horns) was an open-air sanctuary on the western summit of the mountain (Le Glay 1961: 32; Cadotte 2007: 29, 31–5; Plate 12). All datable material from the site, including 600+ stelae, is of the Roman period, demonstrating continuities with the Punic past even in a new sanctuary (Le Glay 1961: 32–3). Sabratha's open-air sanctuary continued into the second century and a first- or second-century bilingual neo-Punic/Latin inscription dedicated to Baal and Saturn respectively found near the city shows the desire to maintain the cult whilst incorporating the dominant official language into cultic commemoration (Longerstay 1995: 842–3). At these examples and others, sacred areas were monumentalised or entirely abandoned during the second or third centuries (Le Glay 1961: 276; Brouquier-Reddé 1992: 29; Saint Amans 2004: 351).

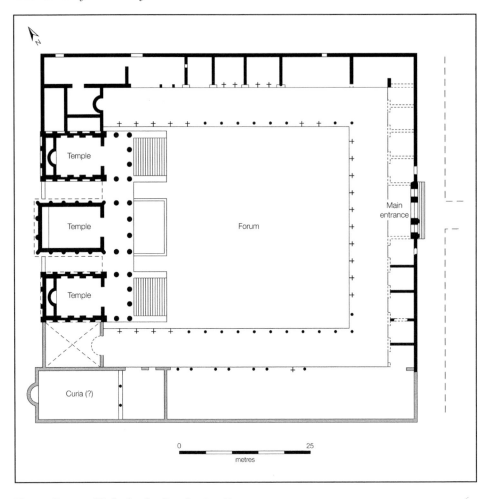

Fig. 3.3 Forum of Sufetula: after Duval 1982a: Fig. 5.

Many temples built in the Roman period had an 'African' character. Groups of deities were often worshipped in the same sacred space across the ancient world but in Africa, instead of providing cult statues with separate niches in a single *cella* (cult room), we often see multiple *cellae* with each deity being provided for separately; we have already seen such an arrangement at Motya (Chapter 1). A famous Roman-period example demonstrating the pervasiveness of this tradition can be seen at Sufetula (Sbeitla) in Tunisia. Sufetula's forum, built in the early second century AD (the gate dates to 139 under Antoninus Pius), has a series of three temples, served by a common staircase, built along the north-west wall of the forum opposite the monumental entrance (*CIL*, 8.11319). The division of the *cellae* in this way is so striking because the location of the temples would suggest that they took the place of the *capitolium*, the temple of the triad of deities Jupiter Optimus Maximus, Juno and Minerva, who were central to religion at Rome and, alongside imperial cult (see below), are the most visible element of 'Roman' cults in Africa. If these three temples were the equivalent of a *capitolium* then the cult was being expressed in a way that made sense to the local community. If the temples were not to the Capitoline Triad then local beliefs were clearly being expressed in a Roman space: the forum.

'Roman' Temples & Cults

The permanence of pre-Roman deities should not disguise the fact that Roman settlers in the colonies established under Caesar and Augustus brought their own deities with them, including the Capitoline Triad. Over the course of the first three centuries AD in many African cities but by no means all, a *capitolium* became an important religious sanctuary (Barton 1982; Plate 13; Figs 3.4 and 3.5). These were often placed as the dominant feature on a forum, although the tendency to think of the major temple on the forum as being a *capitolium*, regardless of whether any evidence points to the identification, has now receded. At Gigthis, for example, there has been a tendency to view the major temple on the forum as being to Serapis, although again that identification is not secure either (Constans 1916: 26–34; Barton 1982: 286–7; Wild 1984: 1779; Fig. 4.3).

Alongside traditional Roman deities the cult of the deified emperors was also introduced into Africa. The provincial cult centre in Carthage seems to date to early in the reign of Vespasian (AD 70–72), and those of Mauretania Caesarensis and Mauretania Tingitana might do so. The provincial cults may have been created as part of an active policy by Vespasian, as the first ruler of a new dynasty, to shore up support (Fishwick

Fig. 3.4 Capitolium at Thugga.

Fig. 3.5 Capitolium at Thugga.

1987: 257–68; 282–94). If so, this is a rare example of a cult being imposed on Africa. At individual cities the incorporation of the cult was an ad hoc process with individuals and cities using imperial cult from the early first century onwards as another way of competing for status and for demonstrating loyalty to Rome and the emperors; some provincial governors also seem to have promoted the cult. In consequence many African cities have dedications to the cult of the emperors, and sometimes purpose-built temples. The vagaries of imperial fortune can be seen in some of these structures and dedications. For instance, a temple to Dis and Saturn was constructed at Thignica under Domitian in AD 93–94, but following his assassination in 96 his name was chiselled out (*AE*, 1992: 1815). Similar acts of damnation are common with Geta, the younger son of Septimius Severus. At Lepcis Magna, for instance, a series of statue bases dedicated to him were removed from public view following his murder and gathered together behind the North Temple on the *forum vetus*, presumably with a view to reusing the stone at a later date (*IRT*, 433, 435–40, 443–4).

Roman cults sat alongside native and Punic deities in most African cities. Their adoption can be seen as part of the complex interrelationship of Roman officials, African urban elites and local populations that have already been much discussed. The introduction of such deities into Africa was often a matter of personal devotion or the will of a city council, but we should not see the absence of any particular Roman cult from a city as a rejection of that deity, much less Roman culture.

Religion & the City

The relationship with the divine was central to the lives of populations across Africa. Purpose-built temples were only one locus in which the connection between god and man was played out. Religious festivals bound the city together with an annual calendar of events; the gods were always present at the city but their festivals brought them into the forefront of the population's minds. Such festivals undoubtedly encompassed animal sacrifice and processions to and from the temples of the gods or other sacred locales in and around the city. Even into the late Roman Empire, at a date when Christianity was dominant, traditional festivals were still carried out and Christianity itself bound the city together through its holy days and processions to the shrines of the martyrs (see Chapter 7). For instance, from the fourth century we have Augustine's hostile account of the festivities of Caelestis that he had participated in during his youth in Carthage (August., *Conf.*, 3.2.2–4 and *De civ. dei.*, 2.4 and 26). At Thugga the physical link between the small theatre and the temples of Concord, Frugifer, Liber Pater and Neptune also suggests the centrality of performance to those cults; plays demonstrating the deity's myths can be expected to have bound the population together at significant moments in the year (Rives 1995: 126–7; Laurence et al. 2011). Another example of the links between religion and 'leisure' comes from Carthage, where Perpetua and her companions were thrown to the beasts in the amphitheatre garbed as priests of Saturn and priestess of Ceres, whilst Tertullian also describes executions in the amphitheatre staged as ritualised performances (*Passion of Saints Perpetua and Felicitas*, 6.1; Tertullian, *Apology*, 15.5). Religion was at the heart of everyday life in the African city but it was emphasised on specific occasions in particular locations.

As in the Punic period, priests were central to city life. The holding of priesthoods was a religious devotion but also a mark of social status and it was diligently recorded as a defining characteristic of individuals on their funerary and honorific inscriptions. For example, from Chusira in Byzacena: 'Consecrated to the shades of the departed, Victor son of Masculus, priest of Minerva, lived for 78 years' (*AE*, 1993: 1721). The relative status of priests can be seen in the mid-fourth-century municipal album of Thamugadi listing civic dignitaries, where the priests appear after those aristocrats of senatorial rank and before the rest of the elite; religious status was worth more than that of *duumvir* (*CIL*, 8.2403, 17,824, 17,903). Holding the provincial high priesthood of the imperial cult was the highest religious honour possible into the third century. Fifteen such priests are known from their honorific statue bases in Africa and four more priests and priestesses are known from the Mauretanias; as with other civic and imperial honours it was important to advertise them when given the opportunity (Fishwick 2002: 187–8).

Part of the priests' importance derived from the need to propitiate the deities with the sacrifice of a specific animal of a specific gender in the correct ritual. Inscriptions such as this from Idicra (Aziz Ben Tellis) detail the animals that had to be offered whilst setting out the hierarchy of deities, with Saturn coming first:

D(IS) B(ONIS) SACRUM
C(AIUS) C(...) PRIMUS
SACERDOS SATURNI AG
NU(M) TAURO(M) DOM
INO OVICLA(M) TEL[L]
URI BERBECE(M) IOVO OVICLA(M)
[NU]TRICI CAPONE(M)
[H]ERCULI EDU(M) MERC
[UR(IO)] AEDUA(M) VENERI
BER[BEC]E(M) TESTIMONIO ...

Consecrated to the good gods, Caius C ... Primus, priest, to the lord Saturn a lamb and a bull, to Tellus a ewe, to Jupiter a ram, to Nutrix a ewe, to Hercules a capon, to Mercury a kid, to Venus a female kid, to Testimonius a ram ... [*CIL*, 8.8247; Picard 1954: 131]

Such rituals helped to bind the city together, with the priests at the heart of the community; this will also be true of the Christian city from the fourth century onwards (see Chapter 7).

City & Country

Urban priests' responsibilities encompassed not just the worship of deities within the city but also deities within the city's *territorium*. The urban community would have been bound to the land by the rites associated with these deities. One of the clearest indications of the importance of rural deities to towns comes from a cave near Thibilis. There the city magistrates erected, apparently annually, stelae dedications to the god Bacax Augustus. The following example from AD 211 (dated by the eponymous Roman consuls) demonstrates the basic content of these inscriptions (*CIL*, 8.18,828):

BACACI AVG SAC

GENTIANO ET BASS

O COS VII ID MAIAS

C IVLIVS FRONTO

NIANVS ET / ANT

ESTIVS PRVDES

MAGG THIB V S L

Consecrated to Bacax Augustus. In the year of the consuls Gentianus and Bassus [AD 211], on the 7th day before the Ides of May [9th May]. Caius Iulius Frontinianus and (ant?)estius Prudes, magistrates of Thibilis (dedicated this stele) willingly in fulfilment of a vow.

The exact ritual which led to the deposition of these inscriptions is not conveyed by the archaeological remains but Bacax's worship was clearly part of the official municipal cultic landscape and ritual calendar. Every year the magistrates of the city presumably processed to the cave, in all likelihood at the head of other members of the community, and placed the inscription in the cave before returning home. The procession linked the inhabitants of the town to an ancient sacred space but also to its own *territorium*. The population's movements to and from the cave would have given the citizens a wider perception of sacred space; the gods were present, effective and needed to be propitiated in and around the town.

The worship of Bacax presumably demonstrates continuity with the pre-Roman past. It is precisely this type of maintenance of past traditions that Bénabou views as being a religious resistance against Roman culture and, by extension, Roman rule (Bénabou 1978: 262). However, the motivations of the communities that continued to express their connection with the divine in old ways are unclear. Religion could easily remain a node around which opposition to Roman rule could coalesce, as it has done in modern North Africa and elsewhere, but there is no actual evidence of this here. It is hard to believe that the magistrates of Thibilis believed that they were being anti-Roman in honouring Bacax and indeed the nature of the inscription, written in Latin with the date expressed in a traditional Roman way, argues against it.

Integration

It is not controversial to state that religious expression was central to city life. What is debated for Africa is how changes and continuities in the way that the gods were worshipped are characterised. Is continuity of worship of a specific group of deities a rejection of Roman power? Or is change and adoption of Roman deities, or at least names for the deities, a mark of deep Romanisation in a city? In reality both change and continuity existed at the same time and, in the main, we should probably view a slow evolution of religious expression as increasing numbers of deities were identified under Roman names and housed in temples rather than having open-air sanctuaries devoted to them, whilst some native deities continued under their old names. As Bénabou himself points out, African populations were able to integrate innovations and external influences into their religion (Bénabou 1976: 261, 263).

The process of integration is obviously complicated and varied from city to city. Roman settlers and veterans in the new colonies of the first century AD obviously brought their own deities with them. For pre-existing communities it is difficult to assess how far garbing a Punic deity with a Roman name actually made a difference to the way in which their worshippers perceived them. Calling Shadrapa, Liber Pater, as happened at Lepcis, would perhaps over time have given the local deity a sense of being an expression of a more universal Mediterranean god. Alternatively it may always have been clear to the inhabitants of the city that their god was a local deity who had always been a part of the city's religious make-up, with his temple occupying an age-old spot on the forum. What we can say is that there was a general continuity of religious belief with the gradual adoption and incorporation of new aspects of cult and Roman deities. This is the mark of Romano-African urban religion at least until the dominance of Christianity in the late fourth century AD.

4

The Flourishing
of African Urbanism

The first century AD had seen the gradual evolution of a Romano-African city-scape with particular concentrations of cities in Africa Proconsularis and in major Mauretanian cities, such as Caesarea, Tipasa and Volubilis. Over the course of the first century we have also seen the development of elites who used Roman-style buildings to stress the personal and collective wealth of the elite and the town, to demonstrate their loyalty to Rome and to provide the city with the facilities necessary for their conception of proper urban life. Additionally we can see the beginning of cultural change as the elites began to express their understanding of the city and relationship with the emperors in Latin inscriptions and through the adoption of new 'Romanised' spaces; these processes continued into the second century.

Intensification

Virtually all of the cities that are recorded as undertaking building work in the first century continued to do so into the second. Over 100 cities are known to have built monuments during the second century before the Severan era, with almost 80 recorded as doing so for the first time. The expansion is particularly marked in Proconsularis. It is not just the number of cities that were constructing which is impressive, but the scale of construction at individual cities far surpassed that which is recorded for the first century. Of course a note of caution has to be interjected here: the number of building inscriptions could reflect a change in modes of com-memoration with individuals or groups wishing to immortalise their generosity in a way that they had not previously done. Alternatively first-century inscriptions could be under-represented due to reuse or destruction during the Roman era. Many cities that record building work for the first time in the second century were not new settlements. Many, including Madauros, Oea, Sicca Veneria and Thubursicum Numidarum, originated as Punic or Numidian cities, which might imply that we are missing first-century AD inscriptions from these sites. For instance, Oea was a large city which constructed a huge arch (Plate 14) during the reign of Marcus Aurelius but it is generally badly understood, in part because its forum, where many inscriptions would have been set up, has never been discovered as the city is buried beneath modern Tripoli (*IRT*, 232). However, we do know something about Oea's second century from inscriptions so it is unlikely that preservation alone accounts for the disparity between the two centuries. Generally there was then an intensification of the building of monuments in the second century but there may also have been a growth in the fashion for erecting inscriptions and some depression of the statistics for first-century building compared to that of the second century.

Of course there are always exceptions to the rule and a few cities, such as Uzitta, Vaga and Zithia, which are recorded as undertaking building work in the first century, are not recorded as doing so in the second. However, apart from Zithia these cities are only recorded as constructing one monument in the first century so they may be sites which could not afford to regularly erect monuments or where the collection of data has not yet been sufficient. Oddly Lepcis Magna, which, as we have seen, recorded prodigious expenditure throughout the first century AD, appears to have built fewer monuments in the second century than the first. At first sight we might suggest that this was because the elite were recovering from vast, unsustainable first-century expenditure. However when we examine the second century building projects it is clear that if there was a drop in the tempo of construction it was very slight. Multiple honorific arches, cisterns, basilicas and temples were all built whilst the theatre was improved (Di Vita-Evrard 1963; *IRT*, 353, 533, 543, 352, 370 and 707, 534 = *AE* 1952: n.177). Indeed the second century marks the moment when the Lepcitanian population opted to build two large constructions that completed the full set of 'Roman' building types that a city might construct: the large Hadrianic Baths (AD 126–127) and the circus (161–162) (*IRT*, 361; *AE* 1952: 177; Humphrey et al. 1972–73: 25–97; Plates 16–18).

The absence of a baths at a first-century city that was adopting Roman-style buildings on the scale of Lepcis is perhaps surprising but, as we have seen, Punic cities seems not to have had a tradition of public bathing (see Chapters 1 and 2). This 'omission' may reflect local conceptions of city life in the first century; bathing in full view of fellow citizens may not have been an activity that was considered normal or desirable. Following this model we may argue that the large Hadrianic Baths marked the adoption of a characteristically Roman aspect of life, which only became a priority for the Lecpitanians during the second century; previously the provision of temples, work on the theatre and paving the city had been more important. It is perhaps important that when the population committed to bathing they did so in a monumental fashion. The main part of the building was over 7000m square, incorporating a large open-air swimming pool (*natatio*) including reservoirs, latrines and a large *palaestra* (an open exercise yard; Plate 17). The bulk of the complex was ordered symmetrically along a north–south axis, which in itself apes the 'imperial' bath houses of Rome, where symmetrical order was used as a harmonious way of arranging space (Nielsen 1990: 87–90, 93–5). The *frigidarium*, *tepidarium* and *caldaria* were all large and arranged in such a way that the progress from cold to hot was a logical and linear path. Only the hot rooms were duplicated, suggesting that simultaneous segregated bathing of men and women was not contemplated; either everyone bathed together or at separate times.

The circus, one of the largest outside Italy, was sited next to the amphitheatre, a kilometre to the east of the city's harbour (Humphrey et al. 1972–73: 27). Circuses were always the rarest major monuments in African cities. A facile argument could be made that Africans were not interested in chariot-racing but in reality there were scant numbers of such structures because: a city only ever needed one (unless that city was Rome); theoretically all chariot-racing actually needed was a patch of flat ground on which temporary wooden stands could be built; and most importantly their size made them so expensive. In consequence, by the end of the second century only Utica, Carthage and possibly Hadrumetum and Thysdrus had such purpose-built circuses; Auzia, Caesarea and Thugga's all seem to date from the third century (Humphrey 1986: 295–336). Lepcis' circus was therefore a sign of wealth and a city's membership of an exclusive club, which in the second century comprised of ancient Punic foundations, the former capital of the Mauretanian kingdom and the regional 'capital', Carthage.

The work on the circus would have benefited from the long level patch of ground between the coast and the hill to the south out of which the amphitheatre was carved and using the hill as banking on to which seats could be set would have substantially reduced the cost of the operation (see Chapter 2). However as Humphrey and his colleagues noted, the chief attraction of the site was the presence of the amphitheatre to which the circus was connected via multiple tunnels and the monumental passageway at the west end of the structures (Humphrey et al. 1972–73: 27; Plate 4). The various paths for movement between the monuments suggest that it was envisaged that beast hunts or gladiatorial combats in the amphitheatre would take place at the same time or sequentially with chariot-racing in the circus. The construction of the circus created a 'leisure' complex on the periphery of the city, a complicated venue where religious ritual connected to the games took place, and where Romano-African ideologies regarding bravery in the face of death and how to justly punish convicted criminals could be inculcated into the young.

The provision of the circus and the Hadrianic Baths did far more than provide Lepcis with the full gamut of Roman-style buildings. They allowed the population of Lepcis to stress their status throughout the second century AD and provided a full 'Roman' cultural package at a time when the city became a Roman colony, adopted Roman civic offices instead of *sufetes* and abandoned the use of the Punic script (see Chapter 2). Clearly whatever attachments to these public aspects of their traditional culture the Lepcitanian elite had in the first century were being set aside in the second. Although, as we have seen in Chapter 3, the populace still adhered to their patron deities and Latin may not have been the dominant spoken language in private (Chapter 2).

Lepcis Magna's building campaigns resulted in it, along with Hadrumetum and other cities, being honoured with the status of colony as a reward for its importance and its Roman-ness, although as Bénabou points out the former seems to be much less Roman than the latter judging by the names of its inhabitants (*CIL*, 8 p.14; Bénabou 1976: 118). Such rewards, with all the gains in status and power that flowed out of them, would have gratified the competitive instinct within the cities' elites. Of course, as more cities achieved the rank of colony it meant that colonies needed to find new ways to emphasise their particularity.

New Cities

The intensification of urbanism was also partly driven by the creation of new communities by the Roman state. We have seen the establishment of colonies in the first century (Chapter 2) and there are few further examples into the second. Communities such as those at Ammaedara and Theveste, founded at bases of the legion (see Chapter 2), achieved independence in its wake with their own elites. It is only in the second century that these cities really started to flourish, constructing the suite of buildings that 'proper' cities needed (*CIL*, 8.304 = 11,529; *AE*, 1988: 1119; *AE*, 1995: 1652; *AE*, 1933: 233). Previously the only known construction at Theveste had been the amphitheatre whose games kept the soldiers entertained. Lambaesis, the home of the legion from the early second century onwards, also developed a city near the legionary fortress, which also became the home of army veterans (see Chapter 5 for the development of the city over time).

Although these cities were founded by Roman power as organised, regularly planned cities, they did not always evolve in such a way. We will examine two colonies – Cuicul (founded under Nerva or Trajan AD 96–117) and Thamugadi (AD 100) – as examples (see Figs 7.4 and 7.7). Both cities were small, regularly planned, apparently sited on virgin land and colonised primarily with veterans. Some commentators have argued, despite a lack of archaeological evidence, for natives joining the Roman settlers on the basis of their non-Roman names or for the cities being placed on the site of pre-existing communities (Bénabou 1976: 115; Fentress 1979: 128–32; Cherry 1998: 43).

Following MacDonald, it has become a commonplace in the study of Roman cities to compare the original city at Thamugadi with the size of the baths of Caracalla at Rome to emphasise the city's small size; they were virtually identical (MacDonald 1986: 25–31). Thamugadi's initial layout was virtually square (317m x 328m) with a regular street grid, its two principal roads meeting at right angles in the city centre, cutting the city into quarters. Cuicul was on an irregularly shaped site, placed on a narrow spur between two wadis, presumably because the drops to the wadis made the site more defensible, but the *insulae* (city blocks) were still placed on to a regular plan of streets that met at right angles (Février 1964: 4). Both cities were walled (Février 1982a: 346). Over the course of the second century both were provided by their elites with Roman-style monuments, including *fora*, temples, monumental gateways and theatres. Probably due to their relatively small size, neither city constructed a circus or amphitheatre although that does not mean that games did not take place in an open space; in the case of Thamugadi the citizens could have travelled to Lambaesis, only 12km away, for special occasions.

These cities may have been laid out on a grid according to the strictures of the impe-rial authorities who would have sent surveyors to the sites. In the case of Thamugadi the city seems to have been built by legionaries under the supervision of their legate Lucius Munatius Gallus (*CIL*, 8.17,842–3 = *ILS*, 6841). However, almost immediately the citizens of both cities abandoned any pretensions to strict regularity by construct-ing new buildings outside of the original cities on different alignments relating to the topography of the site or routes out of the cities. Here 'Roman' populations who had, or whose parents had, lived a regulated life in the army, many of whom had been recruited into the legion from outside Africa or from the cities of Africa Proconsularis, adapted the city to their own needs which did not necessarily intersect with those of the city's founders (Le Bohec 1989: 494–508; Laurence et al. 2011).

Populations at pre-Roman settlements also saw no need to re-build their city on a grid. Cities such as Thuburbo Maius, Madauros and Thugga continued to be adapted to their natural topography or expanded in an unrestricted and apparently non-centrally planned manner. In Thugga's case this is despite the population undertaking considerable building works during the first and second centuries. The ordered, regular city of the surveyors was not what all African populations, whatever their ethnic origins, whenever the cities were built, wanted (Plate 19; Fig. 1.3).

The Written & Writing City

We have already seen that the city, through its buildings, its rituals and its games, inculcated new generations into the ideologies of the populace as a whole through the yearly reproduction of religious festivals and the provision of spectacles, some of which were given by magistrates as part of their obligations on taking office. Another aspect that we have frequently encountered but not fully concentrated upon is the way in which cities became written, Latinised, spaces. Alongside building inscriptions, dedications and stelae to the gods, tombstones, statue bases in honour of deities, emperors and officials all displayed the Latin language to the population (Plate 20; Fig. 4.2). Given the prevalence of graffiti that survives in the particular conditions at Pompeii it is likely that the surviving material was the tip of the ice-berg. Such material tends to be badly recorded but it is clear from the forum of Thamugadi that African cities would have been covered with a range of inscribed material. Alongside the dedications of buildings and the statue bases a sundial seems to have been inscribed on to the centre of the forum (Ballu 1897: 122). There are also several examples of non-official material, including various game boards and a game that the excavator defined as a circular hopscotch game (Ballu 1897: 121–2).

Fig. 4.1 Phallus at Lepcis.

Fig. 4.2 The dedicatory inscription of Carthage's Antonine Baths.

One of these includes the phrase:*'venari / lavari // ludere ridere // occ(isum?) est / vivere'* ('hunting, bathing, gambling, laughing, this is life', *CIL*, 8.17,938). Additionally, in the south-western corner of the forum there is a semi-circle, an image which Ballu coyly describes as a schematic *'sexe feminine'*, a vase with flowers and human figures, and drawings of a phallus accompanied by a heart (Ballu 1897: 122). The phallus as a symbol was often used to bring good luck and is seen at many ancient sites (see Fig. 4.1). Perhaps unsurprisingly Ballu did not include illustrations of the phallus or *'sexe feminine'* in his nineteenth-century publication. The unofficial graffiti along with the six rooms that open off the south portico of the forum at Thamugadi, and which Ballu interprets as shops, and the larger *exedrae* that open off the northern portico point to another aspect of the forum: this was a vibrant, used space, not just a focus for monumental art and demonstrations of power (Ballu 1897: 137).

Cherry argues that the existence of pre-Roman inscriptions shows that the spread of epigraphy does not demonstrate acculturation to Roman ways (Cherry 1998: 83–4). However, by the end of the second century many African cities were covered with the written word on a scale that our evidence suggests the Punic or Numidian city could not match. Additionally the scope of inscriptions in the Roman city was qualitatively different from the Punic period when epigraphy seems to have been largely, although not exclusively, limited to the sacred sphere. Such changes mark a considerable structural change in the way that Romano-African populations could and did express themselves and imply some level of identification with Roman culture on the part of those erecting the inscriptions but also for those who read and viewed them.

Some parts of the population aspired to greater literary achievement than mere inscriptions. Several literary figures, including Fronto, Emperor Marcus Aurelius' friend, and Apuleius, rhetorician and author, came from Africa. Despite this, only two libraries are known in the African provinces, which are incidentally the only ones known in the western provinces outside of Italy. One, at Carthage, is known from a chance comment by Apuleius (*Florida*, 18: 8–9) whilst a small library, occupying an *insula* of the city, is known at Thamugadi, probably from the third century AD (*ILS*, 9362). It is not likely to be a coincidence that the forum of Thamugadi preserves a statue base of Publius Flavius Pudens Pomponius from around the same date. Pomponius was honoured not only because he had displayed great benevolence towards his fellow citizens, but also because of his literary erudition, for which he was compared to a flowing spring, perhaps that to the south of the city which was monumentalised in the third century AD (see Chapter 5; *CIL*, 8.17,910 and 17,912; *ILS*, 2937; Ballu 1897: 125; Wilson 1998: 315). It has been suggested that some of the second-century apsidal rooms on Carthage's Byrsa hill are similar in shape, organisation and orientation to libraries on the Palatine Hill at Rome. However, as the excavators themselves make clear, this is a hypothesis made on the basis of similar room types; there is no definitive evidence to support the suggestion (Gros & Deneauve 1980: 306).

Fentress has argued that the devotion of Thamugadi's population to the written word was partly the product of the city's position at the edge of the Empire; the inhabitants expressed their Roman-ness to the rest of the Empire's inhabitants whilst also differentiating themselves from those who lay beyond the borders (Fentress 1984: 400). Such an argument has the benefit of explaining why Thamugadi might have its own library, but it does not explain why comparable towns across the western provinces have produced no evidence of such structures. Casson has argued that the fact that we only have two libraries in the entirety of the Roman west must be an accident of the evidence, that but for a chance remark in an ancient text and a particularly full excavation (clearance might be a better term) at Thamugadi we would have no evidence at all (Casson 2001: 120–1). Whilst he is probably correct that it is improbable that there were no other public African libraries, it also seems unlikely that there are many that remain undiscovered. It could be argued that cities could only have had one library, making it more likely that they would be missed or that the structure of a library might be confused with a house or a set of rooms associated with the forum. However, it seems probable, in Africa at least, that such structures would have been commemorated with inscriptions. It is hard not to conclude that most towns in Africa did not have purpose-built libraries. Thamugadi may be particularly odd then, an avowedly literary Roman population demonstrating their high culture through a library alongside the Latinity of their official and unofficial inscriptions.

It would be wrong to view Thamugadi's dedication to the public written world as solely the product of a border population however. The *fora*, in particular, of cities across the African provinces, but with particular concentrations in Proconsularis and the area of Numidia, were covered with writing (see Fig. 2.2 and Plate 26). Zimmer's work on the *fora* of Thamugadi and Cuicul highlights the ways in which dedications and their associated statuary could be used to demonstrate elite power (Zimmer 1989; Trifilò 2008). At Thamugadi statuary was apparently grouped according to the status of the honoured individual, with the north-west of the forum largely being the preserve of the city's elite with the other sides, along with the basilica and curia, being used for statues of the emperors. A similar phenomenon has been observed at Gigthis, in southern Proconsularis. Numerically, statues of magistrates dominate the enclosure; however statuary to the emperors was grouped around the forum's focus, the large temple often attributed to Serapis that dominated the forum's western end (Constans 1916: 25–6; Barton 1982: 287). The largest statue was that, probably to Serapis, on the large base in front of the temple; if the statue and temple were to the Alexandrian god his cult clearly dominated the municipal landscape of the city (Constans 1916: 31).

At Gigthis the family of the Ummidii used statues and inscriptions to demonstrate their power across several generations. One Marcus Ummidius Sedatus paid for the construction of the Temple of Concord on the northern side of the forum, including a statue to the goddess (Constans 1916: 49; Fig. 4.3). He had a statue to him placed just outside the sanctuary, as did his son Gaius, dedicated by the other decurions (Constans 1916: 49–50). Gaius also had a statue to him dedicated by his three sons under the forum's east portico, next to the main entry, whilst his second son Lucius Ummidius Pacatus had a statue on the other side of the door (Constans

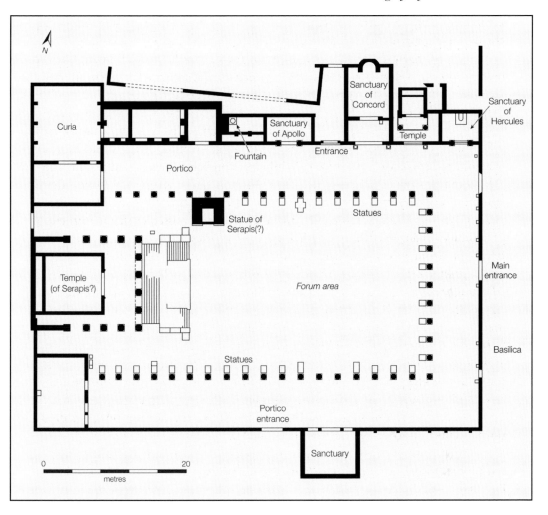

Fig. 4.3 Forum of Gigthis: after Constans 1916: Plate 2.

1916: 50). Not only did the family demonstrate their generosity immediately outside the temple that they had paid for, but their importance at the city led to them being granted the space for further statues. Of course a forum was only one of the most obvious locations for the demonstration of elite power and loyalty to the Empire in the way just described. Other structures where large numbers of people gathered, such as the theatre or amphitheatre, were also utilised (Plate 3).

Writing dedicating buildings, writing preserving details of town charters (mostly lost) or laws (again mostly lost), writing honouring emperors, provincial and municipal officials, members of the elites and the gods, covered cities across Africa conveying both the power and influence of Rome and creating an ever-present literary world for the cities' inhabitants. Given the apparently limited use of public inscriptions in pre-Roman Africa the Roman period saw both a qualitative and quantitative change in the creation of written space.

Populating the City with Marble

Cities were newly embellished with buildings and covered with the written word during the first two centuries AD. As part of that, and usually directly linked to honorific inscriptions, the city's human populations lived alongside ever-increasing numbers of statues – 'the other population' as Stewart has referred to it (Stewart 2003: 118). As we have seen, the forum was one of the most obvious locations for the erection of statues but it was by no means the only place that was used. Baths, markets, the theatre, temples and even the streets were adorned with statues of the gods, emperors and dignitaries, partly to embellish the structures but also as part of the process of honouring great individuals for *summa honoraria* and *ob honorem* payments. So, for instance, the curia at Thamugadi was occupied by statues to the second-century emperors Trajan, Antoninus Pius and Marcus Aurelius; that of Trajan paid for out of public money, the others paid for by a Marcus Caelius Saturninus (*CIL*, 8.2356, 2362 and 17,864; Ballu 1897: 142–3; Zimmer 1989: 84; Trifilò 2008: 113). The emperors would have dominated the building and the decurions who met within it, providing a constant reminder of the power of the Empire, a physical focus for the loyalty of the decurions and the status and wealth of Saturninus. Some of the inscriptions associated with statuary at the city emphasise the power and status of the corporate body of the decurions by stressing either their authorisation of the place for the statue or that the statue had been paid for out of public money (for instance the statue of Pomponius discussed above *CIL*, 8.17,910 and 17,912). Formulae that express this control over public space demonstrate the power of the corporate body of the city across the Roman period. Clearly there is nothing explicitly African in this; such specifications are found throughout the Latin-speaking West. Inscriptions at African cities through their language and proliferation bound city populations in Africa, whatever their ethnic or provincial origin, into a much wider conception of how the city should function and be governed.

The placing of statuary around the city with their number growing over time provided a constant reminder of the glorious past of a city, inculcated due respect for the gods and the emperors and memorialised its leading families. The Ummidii at Gigthis would have gained status through their donation of the Temple of Concord and the steadily increasing number of statues to their members. The statues and their inscriptions helped to provide an institutional memory of the development of the city and the Empire, honouring as they did the elites that had paid for the construction of its buildings and statuary and who dominated civic and religious life through the holding of magistracies and priesthoods. The continued erection of statues, in particular to imperial officials and emperors, into the late fourth century (see Chapter 7) demonstrates the centrality of image and written word to the urban populations of Africa.

Cities of the Living; Cities of the Dead

Alongside the living and the statues there was always another inexorably growing population inhabiting the cities. The dead in their necropoleis were an ever-present part of the world of African populations. Of course this was nothing new. We have seen the provision of necropoleis on the edges of the cities of Punic Africa and continuity into the first century at *tophets*, for instance that of Hadrumetum (see Chapters 1 and 3). Continuity of population often meant continuity of burial place, albeit alongside gradual or even more sudden change in actual burial practice. Certainly Christians' relationship with the dead was quite different to that of traditional practices (see Chapter 6). Obviously as cities expanded burial places that lay just on the edge of a settlement could become a problem and they were often built over. Such discontinuities in the treatment of burial places cannot have been a simple matter of displacing the dead in favour of the living. A shift of this kind is likely to have been more than just a matter of demolishing or building over tombs. It is likely that tombs built over in this way were no longer part of the city's current mental map at the time of their removal. For instance, at Lepcis Magna the theatre (Plate 7) was constructed over Punic graves, the earliest of which was of around 500 BC (Howard Carter 1965: 123). In this case we have an urban settlement where over several hundred years the city's priorities had shifted. Of course any debate (if there was any) over the site of the theatre is lost, so it is impossible to say whether opposition to its placing had to be negotiated, but as construction took place presumably the city council and the funder, Annobal Tapapius Rufus (see Chapter 2), were either unworried about building over the graves or were unaware of their existence when the theatre started to be built.

As with statues and inscriptions, funerary monuments could also be used to define a family's position in society, their domination of the political and indeed physical landscape, their links to ancestral practices and/or their adoption of new cultural vocabularies. Cities in Roman Africa were often ringed by wide belts of tombs with mausolea demonstrating the wealth and status of particular families in death, as their statues and their patronage of games and public building had done in life. These tombs therefore allowed the powerful to impinge on the collective memory of the population long after their death. Monumental tombs, including those of a type referred to as tower tombs, which were at least two storeys high with a pyramidal roof, had a considerable antiquity in Africa by the Roman period so the continued use of such structures demonstrates continuity from the pre-Roman period (Moore 2007: 76–80). The tombs often incorporated statuary of the deceased to preserve their idealised images into the future. We have already examined the mausoleum at Thugga, and other Punic cities such as Sabratha also display examples of monumental tombs that would have dominated the burial areas of the city before becoming incorporated into the settlement proper at a later date (Plates 1 and 21).

Ammaedara, built primarily on the north bank of the Wadi Haïdra on the pre-Vespasianic base of the *Legio III Augusta*, was surrounded on the west, north and east by a great discontinuous arc of necropoleis, including early tombs of the legion,

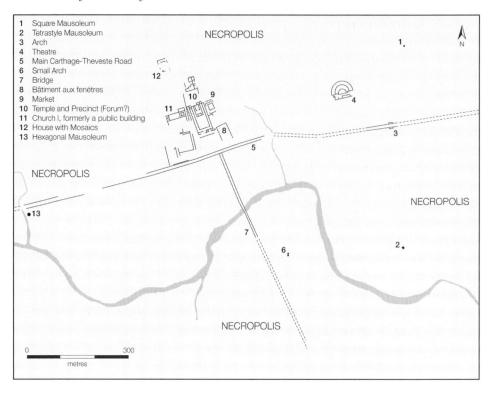

1   Square Mausoleum
2   Tetrastyle Mausoleum
3   Arch
4   Theatre
5   Main Carthage-Theveste Road
6   Small Arch
7   Bridge
8   Bâtiment aux fenêtres
9   Market
10 Temple and Precinct (Forum?)
11 Church I, formerly a public building
12 House with Mosaics
13 Hexagonal Mausoleum

Fig. 4.4 Ammaedara: after Duval 1982b: Fig. 2.

curved around the town only being brought to a halt on the south by the presence of the wadi. Across the bank from the main town a suburb of the city was
also closed off by another necropolis (Duval 1982b: 643–5, 649–50; Fig. 4.4). Within
these necropoleis several large mausolea, the so-called tetrastyle (four-sided), square
and hexagonal mausolea are still visible. These are of the second to third centuries
AD and are 'temple-mausolea': a temple shaped building preceded by a row of columns on top of a high podium (Moore 2007: 84–5). All of these examples are likely
to have dominated not only their immediate locations but also traffic approaching the city on the main roads. Certainly the hexagonal mausoleum was not only
located very close to the principal road through the city, but it was also located at
the point where the road crossed a ravine that led down into the main Wadi Haïdra.
Clearly this location was a prime site at which to demonstrate the prominence of
the deceased and, perhaps more importantly, their surviving heirs who probably had
the structure built. This was a point where traffic was forced across a narrow, clearly
demarcated, space, where the traveller would have had their senses heightened to
their environment more than elsewhere because of its new quality, a feat of engi-
neering with a monumental aspect, a structure that marked the conquering of the
natural world by Roman power (Lynch 1960: 72–83). In such a space the erection of
a large mausoleum would have intruded on the traveller's awareness in a way that it
might not have done if it were located away from the road and surrounded by other

tombs. The mausoleum would have marked the entrance into the town for travellers across generations.

In some ways the examples at Ammaedara are atypical as they are placed within an urban setting. Many other tower tombs were rural monuments, positioned on the borders of estates and overlooking roads (Moore 2007: 81). Just as the examples at a town were markers of an individual's or a family's status, so the rural examples marked ownership of a rural domain and were a method of displaying the wealth of the owners to travellers and other members of the elite. The competitive ethic that marked the construction of monuments within the cities was also played out away from the town in its rural hinterland. Just as the cults of the city extended beyond the urban area (see Chapter 3), so too did elite competition.

One of the most famous of all Romano-African tombs is that of the family of the Flavii at Cillium. The three-storey tomb was built on the family's estate but close enough to the city that it must have made a statement not only about domain ownership but also to the inhabitants of the city (*CIL*, 8.212.60). The tomb was built in the mid- to late second century AD for one Titus Flavius Secundus on the orders of his son, another Titus Flavius Secundus (*CIL*, 8.211). Secundus senior had received citizenship from a Flavian emperor after serving in an auxiliary unit. Secundus' family were subsequently buried in the structure; such monuments were dynastic not just personal. The tomb is notable both for the extreme age of Secundus – he was allegedly 110 at death – and the 110-line poem that adorned its outer walls (*CIL*, 8.213). The poem's composition did not initially mirror Secundus' age, as the last 20 lines were only commissioned due to Secundus junior's annoyance that the original poem did not mention the cock that decorated the top of the mausoleum (*CIL*, 8.213). The cock has been identified as a representation of the immortality of the soul and a guardian animal protecting the deceased on its journey to the afterlife. In itself the cock was a link to the Punico-Libyan past as the bird appears on the inside of tombs of the pre-Roman period (*Groupe de Recherches sur l'Afrique Antique* 1993: 248–9; Lancel 1995b: 222–7; Shaw 2007: 35; Stone 2007: 61). Once the additional text had been ordered it seems likely that the age of the deceased became a factor; the new text seems to be deliberately spun out as it only mentions the cock on line 103 (Thomas 2007: 200). The poem demonstrates the desire of Secundus junior to buy into a self-consciously literary Roman culture but also the family's ability, through wealth, to extend patronage to the poet. In building the monument the family was making a statement about their background and their present status.

Moore has interpreted some of the monuments of the second and third centuries as demonstrating immigrant populations, people with distinctly Roman names rather than Africans with Romanised names, fitting in with pre-existing ways of expressing status and belonging (Moore 2007: 101). Moore argues that newcomers were adopting established patterns of behaviour with roots stretching back over several hundred years; growth in the use of these monumental tomb types was a consequence of economic growth in Africa during the Roman period. Such a reading of these monuments might fit in with many post-colonial assessments of Romano-African civilisation.

It could be argued that native elites were maintaining traditional burial forms into the second and third centuries, with immigrants having to adopt dominant African expressions of identity, rather than locals adapting to Roman patterns of behaviour. However, the provision of inscriptions is an expression of power, wealth and status, as Moore herself recognises (Moore 2007). This very Roman way of emphasising their social status speaks of local communities and immigrants adopting or maintaining a self-consciously literary method of self-presentation in a way that, the mausoleum at Thugga apart, is not really comparable with pre-Roman uses of inscriptions. So we have the use of traditional African elite patterns of behaviour being employed on a wider scale because of economic development, coupled with the application of a consciously Roman tradition of demonstrating status even at death.

Of course the majority of tombs were not monumental; simple graves dominate the landscapes of the dead. Where they have markers they tend to be simple stelae with short inscriptions starting with the phrase *Dis Manibus Sacrum (DMS)*, 'consecrated to the shades of the departed', and which usually contain the name of the deceased, and possibly a dedicator, and some indication of the departed's character. The presence of such inscriptions, whether or not they say anything about the inhabitant of the grave, created yet another written location in the city, a location where the dead were ever-present and where they could be propitiated during visits to leave offerings.

A Halcyon Age?

Traditionally modern historians, partially based on the view of Roman writers, saw the second century as a near-perfect age; famously Gibbon characterised it as the period when: 'the condition of the human race was most happy and prosperous' (Gibbon 1998: 65). Such a statement is clearly overblown even if we ignore the fate of slaves, women, foreigners and the poor; perhaps only a wealthy eighteenth-century British Tory MP could make so bald a statement. In Africa at least, however, the cities expanded and had vast sums lavished on them. Although building on earlier pre-Roman and first-century AD urban models, the second century saw intensification in urbanism as cities were founded and more built monumental structures (and commemorated the fact that they were doing so). The fact that over 100 cities were building during the second century is partly a product of the type of urban network that was present in Roman Africa. As we have seen in Chapter 2, many African cities' territories were small but productive, creating a dense settlement pattern that still provided the elites with the necessary wealth to monumentalise these cities. The cities also saw an explosion in the erection of inscriptions and statuary in the second century, as the elite began to honour the pre-eminent among them and directed some of their wealth into honouring the emperors in word and marble (or less frequently silver or gold). Over time the city, or perhaps more correctly some parts of it, became a preserver of memory, a space on to which elites could inscribe themselves, giving themselves and their families permanence in the city, often over several generations.

Some of the elites commemorated or honoured via inscriptions and/or statuary were of non-Roman origin; others had Roman ancestors who had been settled in colonies in the first century AD. Both groups used a quintessentially Roman media in order to preserve their deeds and generosity to the city in perpetuity. The preservation of their names, in some cases clearly bearing non-Roman roots or traditional titles such as *sufete*, which we have seen (Chapter 2) continued to be used during the second century, did not stop the self same people utilising Latin inscriptions to convey a sense of their status, in some cases their erudition, their family links and their patronage of their city. Even when continuing earlier African traditions, such as tower tombs, new ways of expressing status, such as the incorporation of Latin texts on the monuments, were used to express power relationships within the city and between individuals and Empire. Continuity, even from the pre-Roman period, could merge with the incorporation of new ideas without it demonstrating resistance to Roman power or the use of Roman cultural artefacts, such as Latin inscriptions, demonstrating the abandonment of earlier societal structures or beliefs. Continuity and change could be equally present within African society because individuals and populations were well versed by the second century AD in adopting and incorporating different elements of Roman culture into their societies when it suited them without offending the Roman state or past traditions. This state of continuing tradition overlaid with new practices was also facilitated by complex local identities; we are not looking at uniformly native populations adopting Roman culture but a multiplicity of ethnicities and cultures.

5

A Severan Revolution?

Introduction

This chapter only focuses on a short time frame and has features in common with the periods examined in Chapters 4 and 6. However, the Severan period (193–235), named for the family of Septimius Severus, emperor from 193–211 and native of Lepcis Magna, does deserve its own chapter. It can be seen as the apogee of Roman civilisation in Africa because of the multiplicity of urban monumental construction; certainly some of the most spectacular building projects occurred in the Severan period. The reigns also saw the last real southwards movement of the frontiers.

Fig. 5.1 Coin of Septimius Severus.

It can also be interpreted as an era when increasing numbers of Africans bought into Roman methods of doing things in order to express their wealth, their relationship with each other and authority. On the other hand, it has also been seen as a rupture with the past and a precursor to the problems of the mid–third century.

It will be important in this chapter to not only analyse the content and function of urban building programmes but also to examine the motivations behind them; to what extent was construction a response to a new, African emperor and to what extent was it merely a continuation of previous expressions of Roman-ness in the African city? This chapter will also examine fortress sites, on which the defence of Roman Africa relied, and the settlements that evolved around them. These sites had some of the characteristics of other urban settlements but had a different genesis and actors who could shape the built environment in ways that other city elites could not.

Severan Lepcis

The obvious site to start an examination of the Severan period in Africa is Lepcis Magna, Severus' home city and the object of much imperial spending (Fig. 2.1). During the reign of Severus and his son Caracalla a huge complex of structures was constructed alongside the Wadi Lebda in order to make the city truly 'imperial' in the lavish scale of its construction (Fig. 5.3). Such a set of buildings is not entirely anomalous. For instance, in the early second century, Hadrian had monumentalised the city of Italica, his native city in Spain. Construction at both Italica and Lepcis were to bring their stature up to the level that might be expected for the birthplace of emperors. The Severan structures at Lepcis can also be set alongside the building

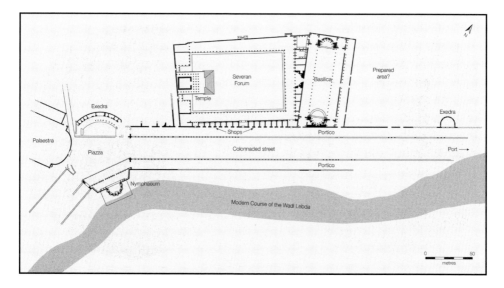

Fig. 5.2 Lepcis' Severan complex: after Ward-Perkins 1995: Fig. 4, 39 and Mattingly 1995: Fig. 6.1.

that the emperors undertook at Rome. The Septizodium, the arch of Severus and the baths of Caracalla were spectacular projects designed to demonstrate the love of the emperors for the capital and its people, as well as their military prowess and stability they had brought.

Although the modern visitor tends to approach the Severan complex by land from the south, it should be considered as leading away from the city's port, which was rebuilt at this time, incorporating new warehouses, perhaps two new temples including one on the western mole and possibly that of Jupiter Dolichenus on the south side of the port, a lighthouse and a control tower (Plate 22; Figs 2.1, 5.3; Brouquier-Reddé 1992: 150–9). The scheme also incorporated an apparently earlier Doric temple on the quayside (Brouquier-Reddé 1992: 125). The new port complex provided a suitable entry into the city for those arriving by ship, emphasising not only the status of the city but also the largesse of the emperor. The incorporation of the temples into this outwardly commercial structure also serves to emphasise the integration of the cults into all aspects of the city.

From the new port facilities the traveller could have turned aside to visit the *forum vetus* but the most obvious direction of travel would have been down the new, wide, colonnaded boulevard created under the Severans, which led southwards from the port. The road itself was vast, 400m long, with a central paved area around 21m wide with 10m-wide colonnades on either side of the road to provide shelter from rain, and more frequently, sun (Ward-Perkins 1993: 67). The width of the road was clearly a statement of the power of the dynasty and the importance of the city rather than a necessity, and it is probably no coincidence that the road was considerably wider than the old triumphal way that led through the city to the *forum vetus*. The Severan road was unable to run straight to the main east–west coast road on its deviation through the city due to the presence of the Hadrianic Baths and instead terminated at a piazza that was framed on one side by a new monumental exedra, on another by the wall of the Hadrianic Baths' palaestra and on another with a new monumental nymphaeum (fountain with statue niches) (Plates 17 and 23). This piazza replaced an Antonine era, 40m-diameter circular space from which another colonnaded street ran southwards to meet the coast road (MacDonald 1986: 57; Ward-Perkins 1993: 79). This redesign of the space monumentalised a crossroads that sat awkwardly behind the palaestra but the two new monuments also distracted the traveller from the change of direction between the two colonnaded streets.

The exedra and the nymphaeum also provided a natural stopping point for the traveller moving southwards through the city and refreshing water, as well as demonstrating the Roman power to tame scarce natural resources. Nymphaea and fountains increasingly became important features in African urban landscapes during the later Roman Empire.

The heart of Severan Lepcis was the new forum complex that lay on the western side of the colonnaded street (Plate 24). Like the street, the buildings were conceived of on a massive scale. The complex comprised of a large quadrilateral forum with a new basilica on the north-eastern side separated from the forum by a range of shops

Fig. 5.3 Lepcis'Temple of Jupiter Dolichenus.

and halls; more shops were on the south-eastern flank and a temple lay within the forum on the south-western side (Ward–Perkins 1993: 7; Fig. 5.2). To the north of the basilica a covered passage linked the colonnaded street with roads to the west of the complex; presumably this was necessary to prevent the forum from limiting move-ment across the city by its sheer bulk. Because the space into which the complex was placed was not a rectangle, the forum and the basilica were not regular themselves. The basilica did not sit perpendicularly across the end of the forum or about the colonnaded street at right angles. Internally the forum was arranged around an open rectangular space of around 100m x 60m surrounded by colonnaded porticoes on its four sides. The ingenuity of the architects was to vary the size of the porticos, shops and annexes to create an illusion of regularity for the visitor in the complex (Ward–Perkins 1993: 9–30). Of course the shops were not just an architectural device to project a false sense of symmetricality; they were part of one of the intrinsic functions of the complex: commerce. Lining the forum and the colonnaded street, they would have been in a prime locality to capture passing trade. Unfortunately there is no evi-dence for those trades within the shops (Ward–Perkins 1993: 25–7).

The focal point of the forum was a large temple of over 30m long and 20m wide which, despite a lack of evidence, is usually attributed to the *gens Septimia*, the Severan family, largely because self-promotion would fit in well with such a huge construction (Haynes 1955: 64; Brouquier-Reddé 1992: 97). Ward-Perkins has taken one of two

Fig. 5.4 Pillar from the Severan basilica.

surviving fragments of the dedicatory inscription ... ONCO ... to possibly refer to the personification of concord but it is extremely fragmentary and cannot be considered proof (Ward-Perkins 1993: 53). Others regard the temple as being dedicated to Liber Pater and Hercules on the grounds that Dio criticised Severus for wasting money on a huge temple to Hercules and Bacchus (Dio Cassius, *Roman History*, 77.16.3). However, it is not clear where 'Dio's' temple was built, and although the dedication clearly masks the Lepcitanian patron deities, Milk'ashtart and Shadrapa, it could have been constructed at Rome. Lepcis' new basilica, however, was certainly decorated with carved pillars that showed Hercules and Liber Pater in various mythological scenes (Haynes 1955: 65; Fig. 5.4). The temple was built on a very high podium of 5.2m which adjoined the back wall of the forum with a *favissa*, a chamber, within the podium's bulk. Unfortunately most of the superstructure has been stripped for building materials since antiquity but it is clear from the remaining elements that it was preceded by 28 steps arranged as a truncated pyramid in front of the podium to extend access to the structure to more than just a frontal approach. The temple had a simple *cella* of about 12.8m square paved in white Proconnesian marble, which was apparently replaced with green marble in late antiquity (Ward-Perkins 1993: 50). The *cella* was surrounded on its lateral sides by a single colonnade and on the front by 20 columns for a porch arranged in three rows, with the front row having eight columns and the two rows nearer the *cella* having six columns each, leaving gaps corresponding to the middle two columns on the front row. It was a particularly richly decorated structure as we might expect for an imperial project. Indeed, the importation of expensive stone: red granite for the temple columns, Proconnesian and Pentelic marble for the column capitals and column bases respectively and Proconnesian marble for the podium paving and *cella* walls, demonstrates the prestigious nature of the project as some of these materials were from imperial quarries whose products were not attainable by just any city (Ward-Perkins 1993: 31, 45–6, 49).

The emperor's act of generosity to his homeland is perhaps not the most interesting element of the unprecedented spending and building at the city. What is fascinating is the way that the elites of the city reacted to Severus' elevation and his gifts, what Wilson has referred to as 'gesture and response', by honouring the emperor with a multiplicity of statues and honours for the imperial family (Wilson 2007: 295, 301–7). Part of the reaction to Severus becoming emperor is located at the junction of the coast road and the 'triumphal way'. As travellers moved along the coast road through the city or into the city from the interior of Lepcis' *territorium* they had to pass under a huge four-way (tetrastyle) arch that had been built over the junction (Plate 25) and may have been completed before Severus' visit to the region and the construction of the Severan complex (Wilson 2007: 295–7). Dedicated to Severus, the arch was decorated with images representing the victories of Severus in the East against the Parthian Empire and the Mesopotamian border state of Adiabene, including a relief of a siege, scenes of the emperor and his family, and of animal sacrifice (Plate 25 and see Fig. 5.5 for similar images at Oea from the arch of Marcus Aurelius). The arch was a statement of the city's pride in Severus but it must have also pleased the emperor

Fig. 5.5 Trophies on the arch of Marcus Aurelius, Oea.

and his family during their visit. It was a permanent reminder to citizens and foreigners alike that Severus came from Lepcis and that his rule brought triumphs for the
Empire. Given that Severus expanded the Tripolitanian frontiers southwards during
his visit, the military underpinning of an emperor's power must have been evident to
all the inhabitants of the region (Aurelius Victor, *On the Caesars*, 20).

Despite the magnificence of the Severan complex, there is no evidence that it
was supposed to replace the *forum vetus* per se, and as Condron has demonstrated the
traditional seat of the city's government was still being used as an arena for display
during the Severan period (Condron 1998: 46–9). A new area, an exedra, was constructed in the southern corner of the *forum vetus* in 198, paid for by a priest of the
provincial imperial cult (*sacerdotalis prouinciae Africae*), Marcus Asper Aurelianus (Plate
26). Several statues of the family – Severus, his wife Julia Domna and their sons –
were placed into this area in 199–200, creating a gallery of the imperial family (*IRT*,
390, 402, 419, 433). The statues were erected by two individuals, Marcus Calpurnius
Geta Attianus and his son Marcus Calpurnius Attianus, who can be plausibly connected to the imperial family as the name 'Geta' was held not just by Severus' son
but also by other members of the family. Additionally, a statue to the god Liber Pater,
designated as the Severan Lar (protective deity), on a grey marble base was erected by
one Pudens on behalf of his son in 198 (*IRT*, 295) (Plate 27).

At Lepcis then the Severan era was remarkable not just for the huge imperially
sponsored projects but also for the response of the elite to that generosity. Despite the
remarkable circumstances of the Severan building campaigns, which must have led
to a constant awareness of Severus' all-pervading influence at the city, the position-
ing of the statues were dictated by traditional patterns of commemoration practised
by the Lepcitani. The inscriptions in the forum exedra were a product of particular
members of the elite's desire to inscribe the Severans into the *forum vetus*, where
emperors had been placed for 200 years. Lepcis displays startling innovation but amid
the changes there was also continuity as the city's population adapted new realities to
the traditional patterns of doing things.

Awards for African Cities

During his visit to Africa in 202–3 Severus not only lavished wealth on Lepcis but
he also further rewarded the city with the *ius Italicum* (Italian rights), which granted
the city the status of Italian communities, exempting it from taxation usually levied
on provincial cities. Carthage and Utica were also rewarded in this way. These awards
to Carthage, Utica and Lepcis can be seen as markers of status, size and the quality of
their urban civilisation, but the immunity from some taxation would have financially
benefited both the city and its elites. Beyond the *ius Italicum* more than a dozen cities
were rewarded with the status of municipium, with at least Vaga, Auzia and Abitinia
becoming colonies (*CIL*, 8.14,395; 9062; *AE*, 1976:703). On a larger scale Numidia
became a province under Severus rather than an area of Africa Proconsularis,

probably demonstrating that enough cities in the region were regarded as established and developed enough to warrant a civilian provincial infrastructure; this change may help to explain the large number of statues to Severus and his son Caracalla (sole emperor 211–217) set up in Numidian cities.

Numidia & Mauretania

Lepcis Magna was clearly a special case. No other city in Severan Africa had such a relationship with an emperor and therefore no other city was likely to gain the level of help that Lepcis did in (re-)creating a monumental urban space. Given that, we will examine whether other cities aped building at Lepcis or created spectacular structures to honour the Severan dynasty. Was imperial aid necessary for a city population to create such huge structures or could the finances available to the elites produce similar results, albeit on a lesser scale?

The Severan era clearly demonstrates considerable building work at many African cities right across the provinces. When building inscriptions from the second and third centuries are examined it is clear that Severus and Caracalla's reigns demonstrate a significant increase on the amounts of building work undertaken during those of Marcus Aurelius and Commodus. As with the second century, this building work encompassed the whole gamut of religious (temples and shrines), economic (*horrea* and markets), leisure (baths, amphitheatres, theatres, circuses) and governmental buildings (basilicas, *fora*, curias) and ranged across the entirety of Latin Africa from Lepcis Magna to Volubilis. Indeed, in many cities it is from the Severan period that the earliest evidence comes of Roman-style building. At Auzia, for instance, on the coast of Mauretania Caesarensis the Severan period, and particularly the reign of Severus Alexander (222–235), was one of precocious construction. Within 25 years the inhabitants (in the person of various members of the elite, including a patron of the colony, duumvirs and a perpetual flamen) constructed a temple to the Caelestii (celestial deities) in either AD 210 or 222, a circus in 227, a market in 230 and temples of Bona Dea and Liber and Libera in 235 (*CIL*, 8.9015 and 20,745, 9065, 9062, 9016, 20,747). Given its antiquity, Josephus believed that it was a Phoenician city; it is hard to believe that the population went from no 'Roman' or public monuments to such substantial works so quickly, especially given the award of the honorific status of colony to the city, presumably a reward for its Roman-ness (Josephus, *Jewish Antiquities*, 8.13.2). Instead Severan Auzia merely seems to be better documented than that of the first two centuries AD. The building campaign was a reaction to the city's new status, a demonstration to itself and neighbouring cities of just what a Roman colony should look like.

Thamugadi, which has been repeatedly used as an example because of the extent of its excavation, is another good example of the extent of building work undertaken under the Severans. Inscriptions and archaeology have demonstrated a range of fairly typical constructions being erected or improved to provide the city with the facilities necessary for a growing city whose elite was conscious of their status and position on the fringes of Numidia, and therefore the Roman world (Fentress 1984; see Chapter 4). Two markets (*macella*) were built at the start of the third century (see Fig. 7.4). One, oddly labelled the Eastern Market by the excavators despite being in the centre of the old colony, was placed in close proximity to the forum and was constructed around two small roughly semi-circular courtyards (Ballu 1911: 13–6; De Ruyt 1983: 198–203). The second, the market of Sertius, built by the family of the Sertii, lay immediately outside the old colony (*CIL*, 8.2398–9; Ballu 1897: 209–18; De Ruyt 1983: 193–8). The layout of the market's surroundings can be viewed as deliberately emphasising its importance and therefore the importance of the family whose very large house was built over the line of the demolished city wall and who may have held property at a site 14km to the east of the city (Ballu 1903: 81–9; *AE* 1992: 1833). The market was placed on the main road through Thamugadi at a natural stopping point just before the traveller passed through a monumental entry, the newly constructed arch (built in AD 203 and erroneously called the arch of Trajan: *CIL*, 8.2368), into the old city. The location was therefore naturally a place where travellers might pause or where they were more aware of the space around them, just as they might have done at the hexagonal mausoleum at Ammaedara (Lynch 1960: 72–8; Chapter 4). It was also located opposite the Temple of the Genius (the protective deity) of the colony, a key location in the spiritual landscape of the city, so it would presumably have been prominent at key moments in the Thamugadian religious calendar. Finally it was set back in its own trapezoidal square so people moving through the city or assembling at the temple would have gathered there and been aware of the tangible presence of the family and their generosity. The inscription carved around the inside of the structure was arranged so that above the six columns in front of the apse was a large letter that spelt out SERTIO, whilst statues to the donor Marcus Plotius Faustus Sertius, his wife Cornelia Valentina Tucciana, his parents and to the donors from their freed slaves, 'peopled' the market (*CIL*, 8.2394–9, 17,904–5). The family were inescapable in and around the *macellum*.

The Severan period also saw the construction of Thamugadi's large northern baths and improvements to the large southern baths (Ballu 1903: 38–48; 1897: 170–88); the so-called arch of Pantheus was constructed in 212–217 (*CIL*, 8.2372); and the theatre was embellished with a suite of statues (*AE* 1941: n.46), alongside the continued provision of honorific statues to the emperors – in this case Severus and Caracalla – in the forum (*CIL*, 8.17,870–1). These structures were dwarfed by the complex of the *Aqua Septimiana Felix* constructed 300m to the south of the city. Built in AD 213 by the city, the *Respublica Tamgadensium*, rather than by an individual (*CIL*, 8.2369–70; Leschi 1947: 87–99; Fig. 5.6), it lay on a roughly north–south axis, with the principal structures at its south end. At over 150m long and 70m wide, the structure was focused on water from a fruitful spring or springs (the *aqua felix*), perhaps located further south, that disgorged their water into its central pool; presumably it was only at this time that the spring was renamed to incorporate *Septimiana* in honour of the emperors (Birebent 1962: 329–30). In the Byzantine period the southern half of the

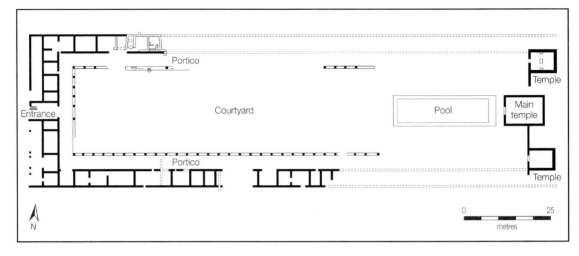

Fig. 5.6 *Aqua Septimiana Felix*: after Lassus 1981: Fig. 9.

structure was incorporated into a fortress and material from the rest of the complex
was reused. This reuse does not help our comprehension of the complex but fortu-
nately several elements, such as the pool and temples, were reused in their entirety
rather than being demolished.

A visitor would have approached the complex by road and entered via the principal, perhaps only, entrance, which lay on the central axis of the complex in the
north wall. Entering the structure, an individual might have crossed the long courtyard surrounded on at least three sides by a colonnaded portico, but in reality they
probably walked along either the eastern or western portico to avoid blistering heat
or winter rain, passing small rooms built up against the complex's external wall.
Eventually the devotee would have reached the long limestone pool of around 22m
x 7m that held the spring waters. The pool, aligned on the building's axis, was surrounded by a colonnade and portico on its northern, eastern and western sides,
whilst to its south rose the bulk of the structure's principal temple of 7.5m x 9.8m,
apparently dedicated to the *Dea Patria*, the goddess of the fatherland, presumably
a reflection of the goddess 'Africa' (Lassus 1981: 50). The principal sanctuary was
flanked by two smaller temples of 5.1m x 7.1m dedicated to Serapis and Aesclepius
(Leschi 1947; 1959: 241). The deities worshipped at the complex were the autoch-
thonous, native, now Romanised, personification of the land plus gods of healing, as
might be expected at a spring (see Chapter 3 for connections between deities and
springs). The abode of the deity was monumentalised in the Severan era because
of the site's importance to the city. Festivals for the deities honoured, and therefore
the movement of ritual processions to or within the complex, probably featured in
the city's ritual calendar. The nature of the cults at the complex, the city's involve-
ment in its monumentalisation and the crucial importance of a regular water supply
suggest that the structure was vital to life at the city, and probably, given the deity
honoured, pre-urban local populations.

Thamugadi, despite lying some distance to the north of the most southerly towns of the province, was still in a frontier area. The nearby Aurès Mountains, which lay within the frontiers of Numidia, contained non-urbanised tribal societies. This lack of integration could be seen as a deliberate rejection of Roman-ness but it has also been recognised as a product of environmental conditions: the mountains, with their paucity of agricultural land, could not support urbanism. The Aurès were also part of the distant hinterland of cities such as Thamugadi, which acted as markets for the products of the upland pastoral economies and transhumant groups from beyond the frontier. Tribal populations probably also acted as seasonal workers, e.g. harvesters, and potentially as sources of labour for major building projects; some of the structures such as the *Aqua Septimiana Felix* were probably far too large to be solely the product of Thamugadi's labour pool (Frend 1952: 68; Cherry 1998: 73).

Fortresses, the Army & Urbanity

The Severan era is an opportune moment to look at another concentration of large numbers of individuals in a quasi-urban setting: the legionary fortress. Severus and in particular his legate in Numidia, Quintus Anicius Faustus, were responsible for the last southwards shift of the frontiers in Tripolitania and Numidia, and the creation of new fortresses (Birley 1988: 216). Towns subsequently grew up around many of these fortresses. Other fortress towns, and in particular the legionary fortress at Lambaesis, were the products of the late first and early second centuries gradually evolving to become monumental centres like other cities.

In Tripolitania several major fortified sites were built leading to the creation of associated *vici* (small towns). One of these fortresses, Bu Njem (*Gholaia* according to *ostraca*, fragments of pottery with inked words, from the site), is important not only as a major fortification designed to protect the agricultural heartland of the Tripolitanian cities from the Garamantes, but also as a tightly dated construction that provides copious evidence regarding power structures and the use of language in the frontier zone (Marichal 1992: 181, *ostraca*, 75). The earliest inscription dates to around 201 and the fort was decommissioned in 263; the withdrawal was part of strategic changes in the defence of the region. The *vicus* survived following the withdrawal and the fortress was reused by the local community with new walls being constructed in places, inscriptions being reused and a silo being constructed in the east gate; the dating for these developments is not entirely clear (Rebuffat 1989: 165).

The *vicus* surrounded the fortress to its north, east and west. It was enclosed within a wall, was generally laid out in an irregular fashion, held merchants' offices and shops and contained shrines to deities – Mars Canapphar, Vanammon and Jupiter Hammon – that seem to have been native deities partially cloaked in Roman garb (Marichal 1992: 98–9; Brouquier-Reddé 1992: 207–10); the latter deity does not seem to have been the same god as the Carthaginian Baal Hammon. The cult of Jupiter Hammon seems to have continued after the withdrawal of the garrison as there are lamps and ceramics of the fourth and fifth centuries at his shrine and Rebuffat argues that the shrine to the spirit of Golas in the camp also continued to be respected (Rebuffat 1989: 156, 165). The worship of the local divinities must have been influenced by the population that were drawn to the settlement, a population that must have been living in the pre-desert already as the cities of the coast worshipped their own blend of Punic, eastern and Roman deities and not 'native' deities (Mattingly 1995: 167–8; Chapter 3).

The fortress, with its barracks and shrines, baths, a population of around 500 soldiers and an elite that made dedications, contains some aspects of an urban site. However, the site also demonstrates the absence of many of the features of and urban change that characterises the cities we have considered, even with the *vicus* alongside it. However, administrative *ostraca* from the fortress reveals the site as the heart of a social and administrative network that was firmly embedded within the local community. For instance, the texts' Latin may show that although Punic had died out in cities' official inscriptions by the third century it was still influencing the speech of the populations from which soldiers of the *Legio III Augusta* were being recruited. The *ostraca* often demonstrate a poor command of Latin syntax and Adams hypothesises that in some cases it might be drawn from Punic grammar, although others have suggested that the grammar might reflect colloquial Latin rather than demonstrating 'Punic contaminations' (Adams 1994; *AE* 1994: 1838). It is certainly true, however, that many of the soldiers' names were either of non-Roman derivation or, in the case of the names Iulius or Aurelius, were likely to have been acquired when individuals joined the army in place of a non-Roman name, and the names for quantities of grain were often those of local measures such as the *selesua* and the *sbitualis* (Marichal 1992: 99–106; Adams 1994: 88). Although it is clear, as we have seen from literary sources such as Augustine, that Punic derived languages were still spoken in the fifth century in rural areas it might be a surprise that the soldiers were so influenced by non-Latin languages given that from the mid-second century AD the legion generally recruited from the African cities, in particular Carthage, and the legionary camp at Lambaesis (Augustine, *Ep.*, 108; Le Bohec 1989: 494–508; Chapter 3). Perhaps the non-legionary units at Bu Njem recruited more widely than from the major cities or perhaps at major cities, below the level of the elite whose names and culture we see in inscriptions, individuals were using Latin that was influenced by other languages and using non-Roman or even Romanised names.

The *ostraca's* content shows the garrison, and by extension the *vicus*, as being at the centre of a large supply network. For instance, some *ostraca* which show little evidence of skill in Latin and use learnt formulaic statements, record the activities of the soldier Aemilius Aemilianus who had been sent to source grain, probably as taxes in kind, and dispatch it back to the fortress carried by caravans of camel drivers (*camellarii*) apparently under the control of individuals such as Iddibal, Iassucthan and Iaremaban; the first name is Punic and the latter two Libyan (Marichal 1992: 182–7; *ostraca*, 76–9).

In terms of the soldiers' lived experience, baths and bathing were as important to an army community as they were to true urban communities. For instance, *ostraca* show work-parties of soldiers being assigned tasks in the baths (*ostraca*, 2–3, 5, 7–13); their construction by the legion in 201–202 was important enough to be commemorated in an inscription and were also the location of a verse inscription of the centurion Quintus Avidius Quintianus to the goddess Salus (*IRT*, 913, 918–9). Both Quintianus' inscription and another from the fortress, by the centurion Marcus Porcius Iasucthan (note the Libyan surname), commemorating the reconstruction of a collapsed arch-way under the Emperor Severus Alexander (222–235), were acrostics, that is the first letter of each line spelt out their name when read vertically (*AE*, 1995: 1641). Neither inscription was in perfect Latin (Adams terms them examples of 'substandard/pecu-liar Latinity') but clearly both centurions, or at least people who acted under their direction, had more grasp of Latin than Aemilius Aemilianus, and expected that at least some of their comrades would be able to understand them (Adams 1999: 109). The inscriptions demonstrate a desire to replicate the 'epigraphic habit' of the cities of the coast in the border area of Tripolitania and, as at Thamugadi, we may be seeing the importance Romans placed on marking themselves off from tribesmen from beyond the frontier. Setting the idiosyncratic Latin on one side Quintianus and Iasucthan were showing off their cultural cachet and the fact that, whatever their origins, they were Roman soldiers and not barbarians, not Garamantes.

A similar attitude almost certainly existed at Lambaesis, the city in Numidia where Africa's only legion, the *Legio III Augusta*, and other military units were based from the first decades of the second century onwards (Fig. 5.7). From that point it was the base of the legate (commander) of the legion who wielded considerable influence within Numidia, which became an actual province during the reign of Severus. The legionary headquarters acted as an attraction for civilians and veterans for over 200 years, creating a small *vicus* next to the camp and a considerable city about a mile to the south (*CIL*, 8.2604–5). The concentrated wealth of the soldiers and veterans, and the deliberate focus of the soldiery's loyalties on the person of the emperor, meant that the display of loyalty to the emperors and gods through the provision of statues and the construction of buildings in their honour could be undertaken more inten-sively here than in most other cities across the provinces.

Various groups of soldiers had an impact on the city. The legate was the pre-eminent figure among these, dominating the legion and the city's built environment; as Thomas has indicated a series of legates constructed buildings in the city throughout the second and early third centuries (Thomas 2007: 80–1). The legates' ambitions were a catalyst for the improvement of the monumental character of the town and as a source of funds distinct from the sums available to a normal city (Fentress 1979: 160). However, the legates were not the only soldiers who placed themselves into the city in perpetuity. Other ranks achieved recognition either as groups or as individuals. Religious devotion could be used by individuals to make their mark, although for sheer quantity it is epitaphs, erected by their comrades as well as their wives and dependents, that provide most of our evidence for the soldiery of the *III Augusta*. The necropolis was full of individuals who were identified by their jobs, for instance *signiferi* (standard-bearers) or *cornicularii* (soldiers dealing with provisioning)

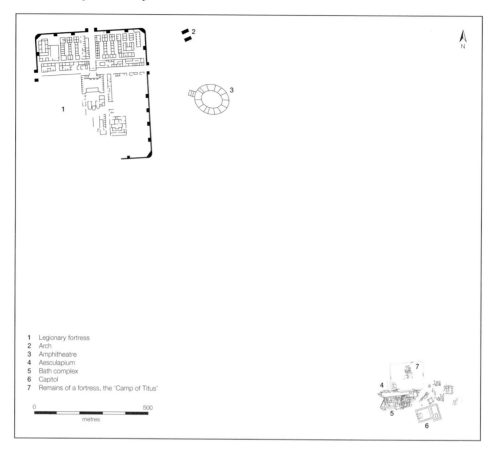

Fig. 5.7 Lambaesis: after Janon 2005: 20 and Blas de Roblès, J-M. & Sintes, C. *Sites et monuments antiques de l'Algérie*, Aix-en-Provence: 180.

1 Legionary fortress
2 Arch
3 Amphitheatre
4 Aesculapium
5 Bath complex
6 Capitol
7 Remains of a fortress, the 'Camp of Titus'

(e.g. *CIL*, 8.18224, 2789). There are also examples of groups of soldiers paying for the beautification of the city, for instance the golden sacred images provided by 50 soldiers of various ranks, including *cornicularii* and a *haruspex*, a divining priest (*CIL*, 8.2586). That the soldiers identified themselves by their job can be seen by the presence of *collegia* (loosely 'guilds') at the city based on the different functions and ranks (MacMullen 1963: 66).

The amount of work recorded in extant inscriptions from Severan Lambaesis is too extensive to go through it in laborious detail (which in itself is indicative of the scale on which we are working), but the whole range of Roman style construc-tions are represented: temples, aqueducts, the road between the legionary camp and the town (conspicuously named the *via Septimiana* – Leschi 1959: 15; see Fig. 5.7) and an arch were all built, whilst baths and an amphitheatre in close proximity to the camp, presumably used by soldiery, veterans and civilians alike, were restored (Jouffroy 1986: 238–83). The legion also provided a large and skilled labour force directed by the legates (Fentress 1979: 161–71). The contribution of the legionaries' brawn to the ornamentation of the city was recorded in inscriptions, including one from the amphitheatre which was 'repaired and embellished' through their efforts (*AE* 1955: 137). The army also provided access to intellect: architects helped to plan important structures such as the roads and bridges that were necessary for regional communication. One, probable, architect is known from an epitaph at Carthage (*ILTun.*, 1085) whilst another was commemorated on a tombstone from Lambaesis, not atypically the word for 'lived' – *vixit* – being misspelled as *vicsit* (*CIL*, 8.2850; Cagnat 1912: 189–90):

> D(IS) M(ANIBUS) S(ACRUM) / M(ARCUS) CORNELIUS FESTUS MIL(ES) / LEG(IONIS) III AUG(USTAE) / ARCHITECTUS VIC/SIT AN{N}NIS XXX

> Consecrated to the shades of the departed, Marcus Cornelius Festus, a soldier of the 3rd Augustan Legion, an architect, lived 30 years.

There are also three inscriptions mentioning '*libratores*' (engineers) from Numidia; two epitaphs and a longer text describe the difficult construction process surrounding the building of an aqueduct, in the 140s and 150s, at Saldae in Mauretania. This work is known from a three-sided honorific inscription describing the career of the *librator* Nonius Datus, which was set up at Lambaesis (Cagnat 1912: 190; Le Bohec 1989: 212, 378; Thomas 2007: 92). These inscriptions demonstrate the presence of specialists and the links between the army and the wider population within and beyond Lambaesis.

Perhaps the most eye-catching element of the Severan building work was the construction of a monumental gate for the Sanctuary of Aesculapius (the *Aesculapium*) that lay at the heart of the city (*CIL*, 8.2585 = 18,091; Fig. 5.8). Developed throughout the second century, the *Aesculapium* provided the necessary infrastructure for those seeking healing from the god (Janon 2005: 38–9). An inscription of the

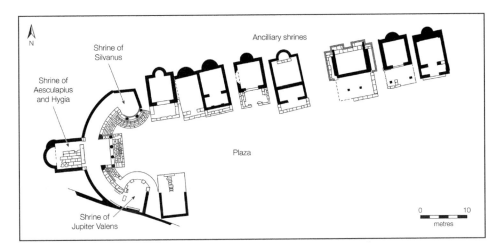

Fig. 5.8 The *Aesculapium*: after Janon 2005: 25.

mid-second century, as well as an examination of the ground plan, shows that the sanctuary's principal temple and its side chapels incorporated shrines to several gods of healing and patron deities for the legion, including Aesculapius himself, Hygia Salus, Jupiter Valens and Silvanus Pegasianus (*CIL*, 8.2579 a, d, e; Cagnat 1909: 86; Thébert 2003: 214); other shrines lay to the east of the main temple. Additionally, several baths were placed to the south of the sanctuary. The water for the complex came from the spring at Aïn Drinn (Birebent 1962: 322; Janon 2005: 35). Other buildings in the complex were almost certainly connected to the healing cult of the chief god: rooms for pilgrims and for incubation (the process of sleeping in the temple to effect a miraculous cure).

Lambaesis may have started as a legionary fortress with the city and *vicus* evolving from it, and it may have had a considerable advantage in the presence of the legion, but its trajectory of urban development was similar to that of many other cities we have considered. There was a gradual increase in construction throughout the second century with major works being completed and started under the Severans.

Conclusions

The Severan period continued several trends that are evident in the first two centuries AD but in some ways it was the culmination of early Roman Africa. Building work continued and intensified at many African cities, with 115 sites having been identified as engaged in building work in the third century compared to only 95 in the second century; much of this change comes from the Severan era. Interestingly the bulk of this difference lies in Mauretania Caesarensis, where 23 sites preserve third-century building work compared to eight from the previous century (based on Jouffroy's 1986 figures with additions). Some of this work dates to the mid–third century but at sites such as Auzia the Severan era appears to have seen a remarkable transformation in the urban landscape. In Mauretania the intensification of building work and an increase in imperial dedications reflects the expansion of the province in the Severan era and a desire to thank the emperor for that rather than the African-ness of the Severan emperors being a motivation for construction. Indeed, apart from Severus' gifts to Lepcis and his connection to Milk'Ashtart and Shadrapa, Romanised as Hercules and Liber Pater, the identity expressed in his propaganda was, as Cooley argues, that of a legitimate Roman successor to the Antonine emperors (Cooley 2007: 385–7). Lepcis is obviously an exception to the general pattern, with the Severans being praised precisely because they were Africans from the city. Lepcis also demonstrates the power of the Roman emperor to warp normal levels of expenditure at individual cities by the application of the Empire's resources. No matter how rich the local elites were they could not compete with such immense wealth.

The Severan period also demonstrates the continued power of local traditions and identities and their careful preservation even if they were expressed through the

1 The Libyco-Punic mausoleum in its setting.

2 Kerkouane baths.

3 Theatre inscription *IRT*, 321.

4 Lepcis' amphitheatre.

5 Earthquake damage: Cyrene's Roman forum.

6 Lepcis' market.

7 Lepcis' theatre.

8 Olive oil making at Thububo Maius.

9 Thugga's theatre.

Left: 10 Temple of Saturn at Thugga.

Below: 11 Zaghouan.

Bottom: 12 Djebel Bou Kourneïn.

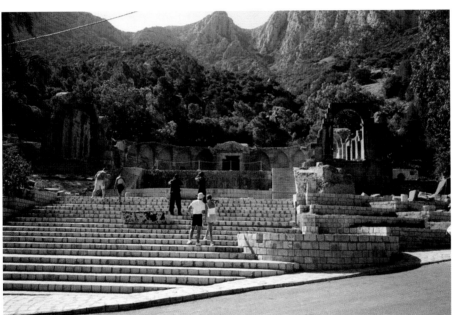

13 *Capitolium* at Thuburbo Maius.

14 Arch of Marcus Aurelius
at Oea.

15 Carthage's largely rebuilt theatre.

16 The Hadrianic Baths at Lepcis.

17 Lepcis' palaestra.

18 Lepcis' circus.

19 Thugga city view.

20　Lepcis: statue base of Septimius Severus.

21 Tower tomb at Sabratha.

22 Eastern mole of the harbour.

23 Nymphaeum and Byzantine gate.

24 Lepcis' Severan forum taken from the temple.

25 Lepcis' Severan arch.

26 The Severan exedra in the *forum vetus*.

27 The Temple of Liber Pater.

28 The amphitheatre of El Djem (Thysdrus) exterior.

29 Cyrene's valley street.

30 Lecpis' temple-church.

31 Carthage: the House of the Cache.

32 Carthage: the Damous el-Karita.

application of 'Roman' architectural styles. At Lepcis the age-old patron deities of the city were maintained and honoured by the Severans within a Roman framework of forum, basilica and temple. This was not a rejection of Punic ways of expressing identity in favour of Roman structures, nor was the focus on traditional deities, albeit housed in Roman-style structures, a deliberate policy of ignoring traditional Roman deities such as Jupiter Optimus Maximus; after all we have already seen the plethora of deities worshipped in Roman North Africa. Instead, Lepcitanian identity that had evolved over 500 years was being expressed in a vibrant, although imperially directed, way that combined the traditional protective gods of the city with monumental constructions that proclaimed the power of the Empire.

Whether the Severan period was good for the population of the African cities is a matter of debate among historians and archaeologists. Birley, in his autobiography of Severus, came down firmly on the emperor having deliberately favoured the region (Birley 1988: 218). Le Bohec in his recent textbook on Africa criticised this view and instead argued that while he was an emperor from Africa, he was not an '*empereur africain*' – an emperor who was particularly 'African' in approach or focus (Le Bohec 2005: 74). Apart from Lepcis a few other cities were rewarded but these honours were not handed out indiscriminately; instead they reflect the riches of particular African cities and their ability to attract imperial patronage through lobbying and their clear commitment to Roman influenced urban culture. Certainly at the end of the Severan era the urban environment of many Africans would have been more spectacular than it had been at its start. Lepcis, Thamugadi and Auzia are only three examples of a wider phenomenon of often grandiose building work that showed off the wealth of the African elite. Severus was a product of second-century Africa, a region with many areas that had long-standing urban histories; his contribution to Lepcis reflects his inculcation into a Roman-African system and then the empire-wide system that associated civilisation with urban living. This situation was not to continue unhindered in Africa for the rest of the third century and in many ways the late Antonine and Severan era can be viewed as a period of over-construction, with some of the welter of building projects designed to boost the status of the individuals and cities causing financial problems for many of them. Even Severus' own building work at Lepcis may have harmed that city.

6

The Short Third Century

South of Sitifis: Resistance or Romanisation?

There is a major historiographical problem with studying the years 235 to 285 as our literary sources for the period are particularly untrustworthy (particularly the *Historia Augusta*, the Augustan History) and patchy but what they do convey is a picture of continual crisis for the Empire as a whole. The sources depict the chaos of a rapid turnover of emperors, frequent invasions from beyond the frontiers, a loss of central authority and a downturn in the economy in part due to social dislocation caused by the political situation. The crisis is often held to have impacted severely on urban centres leading to limited building work before the reigns of the emperors of the 'tetrarchy' (the rule of four emperors) at the end of the third century. In the case of the mid-third century the concept of crisis often meant that buildings and mosaics without secure dating evidence were pushed into the Severan or tetrarchic periods, by archaeologists following historical narratives, as they were perceived to be periods of growth or recovery (Février 1982b: 829; Dunbabin 1978: 30–7). This is a dangerous tendency as once the mid-third century has been stripped of some of its buildings by the modern scholarship then the characterisation of crisis or a society suspended, waiting for renewal, is intensified. In actuality the years from 235 until the tetrarchic era were a vibrant time in Africa, which saw the entrenching of earlier trends of monumentalisation in more cities and across a greater area, as well as changes in society that would lead to new monuments being constructed during the fourth century.

Although dislocation has been overplayed, some parts of the traditional picture are accurate: there was a rapid turnover of emperors at times after the death of Severus Alexander in 235 and many attempts at usurpation were put down. Such violence rarely touched Africa, principally because the region was not particularly militarised so there was no chance that the African army or provincials could raise a pretender to the throne with any real hope of success. The one occasion when a group in Africa attempted to do this was in 238 when the young men, the *iuvenes* (of the elite?), and decurions at Thysdrus proclaimed the proconsul Gordian I as emperor in opposition to Maximinus. Unfortunately for Gordian, the legion and its legate stayed loyal to Maximinus and crushed the revolt, killing many of the Carthaginian elite. Later that year Maximinus himself was killed and Gordian's grandson ascended the throne as Gordian III (see *SHA, The Three Gordians*).

There were relatively few episodes of tribal disturbances within the African provinces during the third century as a whole, especially compared to the European frontiers. However there were outbreaks of violence, mainly in Mauretania, under Severus Alexander in 226–227 (*AE* 1966: 597; *SHA, Life of Alexander*, 7.2–16.4; Herodian 7.4–9) and, apparently more seriously, under Gallienus in 253–262 (Herodian, 7.4–9; *CIL*, 8.2615, 9045, 9047, 20,827, *AE* 1914: 245; 1907: 4). The problems came as much from tribal groups inside the Roman frontier, based within mountain ranges, as from external tribes. It is difficult to be certain whether the violence was reported because they were unusual and therefore worthy of report or whether they were simply the reported instances of a much wider phenomenon of insecurity in Mauretania and to a lesser extent eastern and southern Numidia. Also it is unclear how these problems with tribal groups impacted on urbanism in the region. Certainly most areas of Africa, including the densely populated and urbanised regions of Africa Proconsularis, were spared dislocation caused by warfare.

The need to shore up Roman control over important routes in Mauretania and Numidia was a catalyst to the creation or development of urban centres in the third century, as we have already seen with Thamugadi and Cuicul. In close proximity to Cuicul are Sitifis and a town called Mopth… (the full name is unknown). These were apparently created in the late first century to dominate the mountains and the high plains in this region of Mauretania and as guards against sedentary and semi-nomadic tribes such as the Suburbures, located to the south and east of the cities, who had their tribal lands delimited by the Romans during the reign of Trajan (Février 1967: 60; *CRAI* 1919: 379–87; *BCTH* 1906: 261 = *ILS*, 9382; *CIL*, 8.8812 = *ILS*, 5965). The cities would have acted as foci of Roman culture as well as markets for the region.

In the third century it seems that some native populations in Mauretania to the south and west of Sitifis were sedentary and could be thought of as being urban in some way, although the exact nature of that urbanisation is up for debate. A series of inscriptions (see table, p. 100) could be interpreted as a process of monumentalisation of native settlements. These sites all have inscriptions commemorating their fortification or their expansion during the reigns of Severus Alexander (222–235) and Gordian III (238–244). The inscriptions make clear that the provision of the walls was undertaken under the Governor of Mauretania Caesarensis, Titus Licinius Hierocles, through the '*indulgentia*' (generosity) of the emperors. Hierocles is recorded as having put down the disturbances in 226–227 mentioned above (*AE* 1966: 597; Bénabou 1976: 192–3). These were, however, not just inscriptions that happened to be set up under his governorship. With the exception of those of Sertei, Castellum

Dianense and Cellae, the inscriptions are entirely formulaic. Clearly in each reign the correct wording for the inscriptions was established by a provincial official and then inscribed on to stone to be set up as part of the defences with only the name of the town changed.

Site name	Inscription date	Type of work
Castellum Perdicense	227	Construction
Castellum Citofactense	227	Construction
Aïn el-Hadjar	227	Construction
Castellum Dianense	234	Construction
Sertei	222–235	Construction
Castellum Thib …	222–235; 238–244	Construction/Enlarging
Castellum Vanarzanense	238–244	Enlarging
Lemellef	238–244	Enlarging
Cellae	243	Construction

What does the erection of these wall circuits tell us about the sites and the nature of urbanism in the region? The fortifications of these *castella* are not the same as those of earlier cities. In the first and second centuries AD wall circuits were the preserve of high-status sites, usually Roman colonies or important *municipia* (Chapter 2), but clearly these settlements did not receive fortifications because of their status or as an imperial favour to monumentalising settlements; even if some of the sites such as *Castellum Citofactense* were of some size they were not a rival to Thamugadi, let alone a city such as Caesarea (Matthews 1976: 164). They are less about the status of the city and more clearly about protecting the agriculturally wealthy region around Sitifis, and in particular the imperial estates (see Chapter 2), from attack (Bénabou 1976: 190–1; Fentress 1990). Whether the walls were expected to be needed is less important than the statement they made about Roman power. A wall circuit, with an accompanying Latin inscription, gave a sense of permanence to the Roman occupation in the region and informed both the inhabitants of the settlement and outsiders of the power of Rome.

The wall circuits in and of themselves do not confirm these sites as cities in the mould of Carthage or even Thugga. Although clearly more than forts due to the size of the ruins and whilst the inscriptions suggest a corporate identity on the part of the inhabitants, these sites have yet to yield any further indications of monumental building work. The one exception to this is Lemellef, which undertook work on its water supply between AD 246 and 249, but Lemellef was not a *castellum* (*CIL*, 8.8809 = *ILS*, 5785). It is possible that this situation would change substantially with excavation but at the moment it appears that walls were the defining monumental characteristic of these places. Defence and the projection of Roman power seem to be the raison d'être for these constructions rather than inhabitants demonstrating their Romanness through city-wall construction. This and the formulaic inscriptions mean that it is dangerous to assume that the inhabitants of the *castella* were really adopting Romano-African methods of displaying status and wealth. These inscriptions tell us little about the language spoken at the settlement and the extent to which the inhabitants identified with 'Roman' culture. To complicate matters Février has suggested that '*castellum*' may be more of a legal definition of a group of people that had a walled place where they could gather, rather than a place where they lived, whilst Bénabou would follow the idea of the walled *castellum* as a refuge for a group of people in times of danger (Février 1964: 40; Bénabou 1976: 190–1). Both ideas are plausible although the large wall circuits, the presence of inscriptions and the fact that they were enlarged might suggest that they were more than a simple refuge.

Building in Third-Century Africa

Away from the Mauretanian *castella* it is clear that there were reductions to the amount of building and restoration work that was being undertaken during the third century compared to the Severan period. Figure 6.1 demonstrates a decline in the number of inscriptions recording new buildings or repair to buildings per year (averaged across a reign or group of reigns) from 5.75 inscriptions per year under Severus (193–211) and 4.83 under Caracalla (211–217) to close to one or fewer in the 50 years between 235 and 285, with the exception of a slight increase under Gordian III (238–244). It is tempting to see this as a response to the troubled times of the third century, either because of a reduction in wealth caused by economic difficulties or because of a loss of cachet to be gained by erecting a building with an emperor's name on it when they were likely to be short lived anyway.

There are other ways to view these changes. First, it is important to note that it is building work that was commemorated by inscriptions rather than building work attested archaeologically. What we could be seeing here is a reluctance to commission the erection of the inscription rather than a decline in building work per se, although given the resurgence of commemorative inscriptions in the fourth century this may

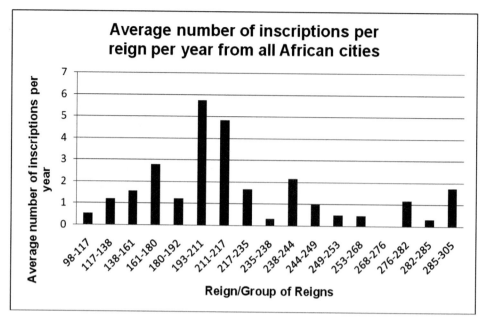

Fig. 6.1 African building inscription rates.

be unlikely. Second, rather than seeing it as a decline from the Severan era, the rate of construction in the third century could be interpreted as a return to levels of work undertaken during the early second century. On this model it is the late Antonine and Severan era that is the anomaly, indeed an unsustainable aberration, rather than the third century; Lepcis, which we will discuss later in the chapter, could be seen as the archetypal example of cities retrenching in the face of changed circumstances.

Beyond the group of settlements near Sitifis very few other cities are documented as constructing walls in the third century. The army was clearly enough of a guarantee of security to mean that in most areas walls were not considered a necessity for defence nor, given that Carthage remained un-walled, a monument that defined urban civilisation. The fact that small sites whose urban credentials were questionable might have wall circuits could also be related to the lack of wall construction; once the *castella* were walled they ceased to differentiate major cities from other settlements. For this reason other cities may have chosen to pursue the construction of other buildings and, increasingly in the third century, baths and temples, rather than seek to construct walls.

Religious Evolution?

If we look at the types of buildings commemorated as being constructed or reconstructed in the post-Severan third century, out of 50 structures that can be securely dated to a reign or to the second half of the third century, 18, over a third of the total, were temples. As in previous eras a substantial group of the temples were to fertility deities such as Saturn, Caelestis, Tellus and Frugifer, and of course deities such as Pluto and Neptune might also mask local fertility gods. This construction work demonstrates the continued importance of ensuring favourable harvests through the continued adoration of the gods even in an era of reduced outlay on monumental structures. Given the centrality of agricultural produce to the fortune of the African provinces this concentration should not be a surprise.

The core nature of the fertility deities to African societies over the long-term means that it is even more surprising that none of the temples that had work done on them under the emperors of the tetrarchy (285–305) or later were to Saturn or fertility deities. Equally, stelae to the deities stop being erected in their precincts. This phenomenon has been remarked on before and has often been attributed to growing Christianisation and therefore rejection of the deities or due to an anti-Roman rejection of the progressive 'Romanisation' of the cults (Frend 1952: 104–6; Picard 1984: 27). We have already critiqued the concept of deep divides between Roman and non-Roman and the idea of Romanisation, but some examination of the model is important. The latest securely dated inscriptions to Saturn are from the earliest years of the fourth century. For instance an altar from Thamallula dedicated by the priest Rodius Lucius to Saturn and Ops dates to 302 (*AE* 1995: 1788); perhaps in this case it made a difference that this Saturn may have been the Italian deity, given that he was being paired with Ops, rather than the traditional African Saturn (see Chapter 3). The third- and early fourth-century literary sources point to growing Christian communities, some of which were capable of reacting aggressively to the Great Persecution, between 303 and 311, under the emperors of the tetrarchy (*Proceedings before Zenophilus*, 16–7). However, it is difficult to produce a coherent picture from different sources or to absolutely confirm Frend's model. Christian sources emphasise Christian numbers, either deliberately to show the strength of the faith, or incidentally through their general focus on Christianity, but despite this there are hints in the fourth-century literature of continued pagan practice and reverence for Saturn and Caelestis (see Chapter 7). It is also difficult to assess when the temples of Saturn went out of use. Several sanctuaries were destroyed but when exactly and in what circumstances is unclear; Le Glay's volumes on the temples of Saturn rarely give dates for dereliction or destruction because of a lack of stratigraphic excavation (Le Glay 1961–66). The disappearance of stelae might demonstrate a loss of faith among the god's adherents but, as with the changes in sanctuary type in the second and third century, it might just demonstrate changes in how Saturn cult was conducted.

The third century in Africa saw the growing importance, at least in our literary evidence, of the sect known as Christians. However, if it is difficult to know what the archaeological changes in Saturn cult mean then it is virtually impossible to assess the third-century African Christian community from archaeological material; we do not have one example of an African Christian building from before Emperor Constantine the Great's conversion to the faith in the first decades of the fourth century. Clearly the

Fig. 6.2 Coin of Decius.

Fig. 6.3 Coin of Diocletian.

Christian community were meeting somewhere, after all we have literary evidence of these meetings, and it is likely that some structures were like the well-known house church found at Dura-Europos in Syria that dated to before the mid-250s (Welles 1967, 12–55). A converted house with a room set aside for meetings and a baptistery was all that a congregation needed. The ephemeral nature of the 'Christian' elements at Dura and the likelihood that such structures may have been demolished to make way for larger churches in the fourth and fifth centuries means that even if examples of house churches had been discovered in Africa it would be difficult to satisfactorily define them as such. Such structures are traditionally viewed as being small to escape detection by the authorities but a quick perusal of the martyr literature from the persecutions under Decius (249–251), Valerian (257–260) and the Great Persecution (303–311) suggests that the authorities rarely had trouble locating Christian leaders or their bases (e.g. *Proceedings before Zenophilus*, 16–7; Fig. 6.2). Indeed, papyri from

Oxyrhynchus in Egypt demonstrate that in the late third century streets were named after churches (*P.Oxy.*, 1.1898, No 43 verso, White 1997: 164–6). Similarly, the main church at Nicomedia, the residence of the emperor Diocletian, the lead emperor in the tetrarchy, was large and prominent enough to merit total destruction whilst the emperor watched from his palace during the Great Persecution (Fig. 6.3; Lactantius, *On the Deaths of the Persecutors*, 11–3). African Christian meeting places could have been large or small but we are currently virtually entirely ignorant of the nature of these structures.

We are almost as ignorant about third-century Christian burial as we are about Christian meeting places. It is likely even in the third century that not all Christians would have been buried in a recognisably 'Christian' way. Many Christians would have been buried alongside and/or in a similar manner to non-Christians who may have comprised their families and friends. Additionally Christian numbers were comparatively small, probably well into the fourth century so unless their burial practices were particularly diagnostic, Christians would be swamped in the archaeological record by non-Christian remains. As a result there are very few third-century remains that can be defined as Christian.

Our literary sources demonstrate that African Christians had begun to create their own sacred burial areas on the fringes of some cities by the mid- to late third century. Tertullian indicates in his treatise to Scapula (pre-213), the proconsul of Africa, that the burial of Christians was a matter of concern for Christians and wider society (Tertullian, *To Scapula*, 3.1). Tertullian mentions that non-Christians objected to Christian *areae* (burial areas) during the proconsulship of Hilarian. It is hard to see why Tertullian would invent this opposition even if he, as an enthusiastic Christian convert, was hardly a disinterested observer. What is unclear is the nature of the dispute. Was the problem specifically the creation of Christian funerary enclosures or was the burial of Christians per se an issue? The use of *areae* certainly implies the former and he does not indicate that Christians were being denied burial when he was writing. It may have been the creation of a conspicuously Christian space that caused the protests, perhaps when Christians were buried alongside their families or within normal necropoleis they were less obviously undermining the correct social order (see below for archaeological evidence supporting this supposition). Conspicuous separation from society could have played a part in the authorities seizing Christian cemeteries during the persecution of Valerian although the main motivation was the seizure of all corporate Christian property rather than a targeted assault on burial places (Eusebius, *History of the Church*, 7.13.3).

The literary evidence also suggests the beginnings of a third-century African martyrological culture, where some Christians were deliberately buried near the martyrs, whose sacrifice gave them special sanctity among Christian congregations. Presumably for this reason, following Saint Maximilian's execution in 295 at Theveste (although when the *Passion of Maximilian* was written is not clear) Pompeiana, a fellow Christian, had his body shipped 300km from Theveste to Carthage, where he was buried next to St Cyprian, the pre-eminent African martyr. When Pompeiana subsequently died 13 days later she was also buried nearby (*The Passion of St Maximilian of Tebessa*, 3). So the textual tradition demonstrates the formation of a sanctified burial area (burial *ad sanctos*) where the martyred dead and the wider Christian community could be buried. The large cemetery basilicas that grew up on these sacred sites at Carthage in the fourth and fifth centuries are the culmination of this third-century trend (see Chapter 7).

The only excavated series of catacombs that can be compared to the famous examples from Rome or Syracuse are those discovered at Hadrumetum in the early twentieth century. The catacombs of the Good Shepherd, Agrippa, Hermes and Severus (the names are arbitrarily defined by art work or individuals buried at the sites) seem to show mixed non-Christian and Christian burial places that may start in the third century, although the exact dates are not clear. Several of the catacombs were in use by the fourth century and beyond, although no work has really been done on the dating of ceramics from the tombs such as lamps, further than identifying them as 'Christian', 'pagan' or 'Roman' on the basis of their iconography (Leynaud 1922). One of the epitaphs in the catacomb of Severus was to a centurion, Quintus Papius Saturninus Julianus, who served with the second Parthian legion which was only created under Septimius Severus. The exact date of the epitaph is unknown but Leynaud argued that it is likely to date to the third to early fourth century as after the mid-fourth century a legion with that name was based in the east of the Empire rather than its original home in nearby Italy (Leynaud 1922: 11–5; 405).

The catacombs themselves display a range of material that could be considered Christian, non-Christian or either, despite the tendency of the Archbishop Leynaud's report to concentrate on the Christian evidence. Invoking Christ or the Christian God obviously demonstrates religious adherence but there are few such examples in the Hadrumetum catacombs. Statements of living or resting *in pace* – in peace – can be seen as Christian. Several epitaphs contain variations or abbreviations of *Dis Manibus Sacrum* (see Chapter 4) traditionally seen as diagnostic of a 'pagan' grave. In a similar vein the presence on an epitaph of the date of death, for instance *V kalendas Martias* – the fifth day before the calends of March – has been seen as a Christian practice; there are 55 attested examples of this practice on tombs from the catacombs. Using this method of differentiation the catacomb of Agrippa, which has many versions of *DMS* but no dates, could be considered pagan whilst the others, and in particular the huge catacomb of the Good Shepherd which has 38 attested dated epitaphs could be considered Christian. However, methods of divining faith using *DMS* or dates of death have been criticised in recent years and it has been shown that such hard and fast separation between Christian and non-Christian epitaph forms did not exist, with some inscriptions showing a mixture of elements (Février 1978: 266–9; Johnson 1997: 49). Mixed use of cemeteries seems to have been the norm well into the Christian era due to the practice of burying family and *collegium* members together. At Hadrumetum this may explain the presence of 'pagan' and 'Christian' lamps in the catacomb of the Good Shepherd or a Christian lamp, defined by Leynaud through the decoration of a palm and lamb, in the catacomb of

Agrippa (Leynaud 1922: 341). Additionally, the entrance of the catacomb of the Good Shepherd was amidst an earlier, presumably 'pagan' necropolis (Leynaud 1922: 48–9). So these may not be 'Christian' and 'pagan' catacombs but catacombs for the population of Hadrumetum, which over time were increasingly Christian. Alternatively and additionally, those creating the epitaphs (and of course epitaphs reflect the attitudes and beliefs of the commemorators rather than the commemorated) may have deliberately used terms that appealed to their own beliefs but which could be considered more typical of other religious communities. We have already seen this syncretism between Carthaginian, Libyan and Roman religious practice and belief and it played a major part in religious expression in late antiquity; Christian and pagan were not as separate as we might expect.

Traditional Building

After temples, baths appear to have been the most popular monument to reconstruct or build in third century Africa, with six examples being dated to after the Severan era with various degrees of certainty, another four sets having been dated to a nebulous third century. The so-called Licinian Baths at Thugga, traditionally dated to the reign of Gallienus (253–268) on the basis of a fragmentary inscription was used to show continuity of urban traditions at the city throughout the third century (Fig. 6.4). However a re-reading of the inscription of these axially aligned baths, provided with symmetrical sets of rooms around a central hall, has convincingly re-dated them to the reign of Caracalla (Thébert 2003: 177). Perhaps one of the most substantial works undertaken on bathing complexes in the middle of the fourth century is at Volubilis. There an inscription of Gordian III (238–239) commemorates a major reconstruction of a '*domus cum balineo*' (house with bath) by the procurator (governor) of Mauretania Tinigitania, Marcus Ulpius Victor (Thouvenot 1949: 47–8; Thébert 2003: 279–80; *IAM*, 2, 404). Given that the building that the inscription was found in was the largest structure at the city, it is most likely that this so-called 'Palace of Gordian' (74m x 69m) was actually the governor's palace (Fig. 6.5). The large, L-shaped bath complex within it (49.5m x 37.5m in its largest dimensions), which perhaps occupied a quarter of the ground floor space of the complex, was therefore the governor's private baths rather than a public structure per se, presumably only open to the governor, other high ranking officials, their families and guests. The complex has an almost linear arrangement where the bather would have progressed through vestibules where they would have de-robed, through a cold room (*frigidarium*) with two pools, to either a colonnaded courtyard that might have functioned as a *palaestra*, or into a suite of three 'hot' rooms that culminated in a pool. These baths were not the product of Volubilis' wealth but of the governor's determination to have a luxurious residence.

Works on the water supply, which could be connected to the provision of baths as well as fresh drinking water, took place at several cities. Thamugadi had a new

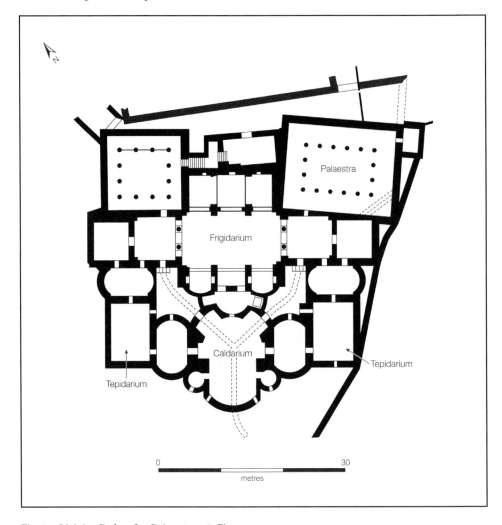

Fig. 6.4 Licinian Baths: after Poinssot 1958: Fig. 5.

fountain constructed at it, apparently after 244 (Boeswillwald et al. 1904: 318); Lemellef (246–249), Tiddis (251) and Thysdrus (second half of the third century) all had works undertaken on their water supply (*CIL*, 8.8809, *ILAlg.*, 2.3596 and *ILS*, 5777); and at Lambaesis an aqueduct described in the relevant inscription as the '*aqua titulens*' was constructed under the emperor Probus (276–282) (*CIL*, 8.2661 = *ILS*, 5788). Other inscriptions and archaeological evidence combines to suggest that building work on public buildings was still considered essential throughout the third century at many cities. Amphitheatres, triumphal arches, forums, porticoes, basilicas and *curiae* were all constructed during this period (the theatre is an odd omission from this list) but this was work was at lower rates than in the Severan period.

Lambaesis continued to be improved even after the disbandment of the legion under Gordian III as punishment for their role in defeating his grandfather. Presumably the periodic presence of a governor at the city would have compensated

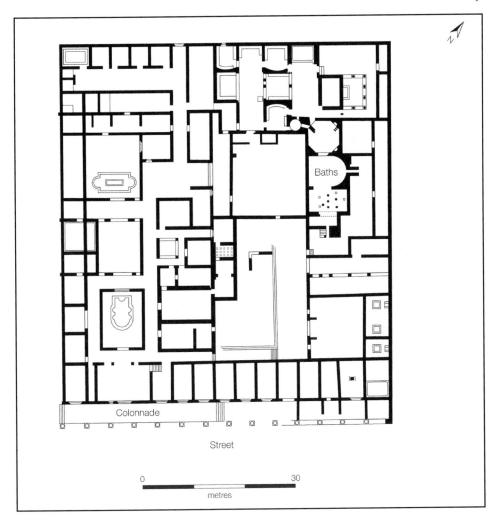

Fig. 6.5 'Palace of Gordian': after Thébert 2003: Plate 136.

for the loss of the legionary legate. In the post-Severan era a *septizonium* (a monumental fountain), the governor's palace, a baths and a temple, possibly to Silvanus, were all restored (*CIL*; 8.2657 = 18,105 = *ILS*, 5626; *CIL*, 8.2729; *AE* 1971: 508; Leschi 1959: 173). The fact that these works were all restorations might suggest that there were not funds available to construct new monuments. Duncan-Jones, for instance, keeps reconstructions out of his building statistics because they could cost considerably less than a new building, however a total refurbishment of a major complex could cost considerably more than the construction of a new shrine so it does not seem useful to divide building work in this way particularly when we are examining attitudes to the maintenance of the monumental city (Duncan-Jones 2004: 34 n.62). The work undertaken at Lambaesis clearly indicates that the governor in particular but presumably a wider constituency believed that it was important to maintain and improve on the city's glory.

Clearly Volubilis and Lambaesis were still being monumentalised in the mid-third century. However there were special factors at work at these cities. Cities with access to high-ranking imperial officials had access to funds and influence beyond that available to most communities. Other cities were also building but clearly the intensity of recorded construction had slackened compared to the Severan period.

Economy

As with construction it is easy to take a few examples and generalise too much about the economy in Africa. There are, however, indications from several cities of economic problems that impacted on city populations' ability to replicate the spending of earlier centuries. Such problems are despite the continuing and indeed growing importance of African exports to the wider Mediterranean. Olive oil from Tunisia, for example, came to dominate the imports into Rome and Ostia after the early second century and this continued in the third century. In addition to the Tunisian produce Tripolitania, as we have seen, was a key part of the Mediterranean oil trade across the Roman imperial (MacMullen 1988: 11–15; Mattingly 1988a: 54–6). Given these trends it is perhaps surprising that several cities with large productive hinterlands, three of them major ports, all demonstrate economic problems during the course of the third century.

Excavation at both Thysdrus and Hadrumetum seems to show the cities contracting or at least retrenching in the aftermath of Gordian I's revolt. It is, however, unclear to what extent these changes are due to the reprisals enacted against the elite, and in particular the *negotiatores* (exporters) of the region by Capellianus, Maximinus' legionary legate. To complicate matters the evidence from the two cities seems to show divergences in response to these problems. At Thysdrus there is evidence of some houses being destroyed and then later rebuilt over a destruction level that contains coinage and pottery fragments from around 238 (Foucher 1961: 12, 22). Other houses in the southwestern quarter were apparently abandoned after the mid-third century and some were subsequently used for a necropolis (Foucher 1964: 315 n.1306; Duliere et al. 1996: 7). For instance, a mosaic depicting amphitheatre scenes in room 24 in the 'Sollertiana Domus' (the house's name in a mosaic inscription) was cut through by six graves, including that of a child, which contained a large red ceramic plate, a late second- to early third-century bowl, a lamp dating to between 250 and 300, and a small dish; the material suggests a mid- to late third-century date for the grave (Duliere et al. 1996: 4–7, 28). However, next door in the House of the Peacock new mosaics were laid during the late third or fourth centuries before, at an unknown date, that house too had graves placed in it; so we should not envisage a uniform process of abandonment (Duliere et al. 1996: 39, 48, 52). Even as some houses were abandoned it seems that the imperial authorities took a hand in embellishing Thysdrus as the scale of the building is probably beyond the capabilities of a newly punished city. The building work was almost certainly related to Gordian III's elevation to the throne (Bomgardner 2000: 148; Plate 28; Fig. 6.6, 6.7); a demonstration of gratitude to a city that had suffered on his family's behalf would sit well with the ideology of an emperor caring for his people and would echo the great works of earlier emperors such as Severus.

Although not accurately dated, a vast new amphitheatre appears to have been built at the city in the mid-third century to replace an earlier structure. One of the best-preserved amphitheatres in the Roman world, the three storeyed, 147.9m x 122.2m structure, could have seated around 40,000 people (Bomgardner 2000: 175), probably far more than would have been able to attend most events held there. Practicality was clearly less important than the statement that it made; if practicality had been the prime concern then the earlier '*amphitheatrum minus*' would have been refurbished even if damaged during the revolt. Beyond the amphitheatre a circus, large bath building and a palace-type residence have been plausibly linked to a Gordianic embellishment of the city, although they are undated (Slim 1976: 919–20; Bomgardner 2000: 128). Despite the focus on Thysdrus, the new amphitheatre was never completed, possibly due to the drying up of imperial support after Gordian's death, and an inability of the city's inhabitants to support such a project rather than a decline as such in the city's fortunes. As we have seen at Lepcis, imperial patronage did not have to have an economic logic.

At Hadrumetum houses in the northern quarter were colonised by graves from the later third century onwards, creating a new cemetery zone; coins in graves in the House of the Peacock and near the mosaic of Virgil date to the reigns of Tetricus (270/1–3) and Claudius II (268–270) respectively (Foucher 1964: 315–6). Foucher has plausibly argued that the events of 238 could have forced the *negotiatores* to move to safer ports, shifting the export route in favour of other cities and leading to the abandonments, but there is little actual evidence for this being the cause of the change (Foucher 1964: 321). Given the likely time lag between coining and deposition there seems to be at least 40 years between Capellianus' reprisals and the creation of the graves, this seems too long to establish a definitive causative link between revolt and abandonment. The houses could have been abandoned due to an area becoming unfashionable or peripheral to

Fig. 6.6 Coin of Gordian III.

Fig. 6.7 The amphitheatre of El Djem (Thysdrus) interior.

the rest of the city and it is also dangerous to assume that because one area was abandoned there was widespread change at a city level. The fact that at the end of the third century Hadrumetum was made the capital of the new province of Byzacena suggests that it was still a thriving and wealthy city (Lepelley 1981: 262).

Further south there is some evidence that all was not well in Lepcis and Sabratha. In the case of Lepcis there is a danger of assuming that the Severan era is the yardstick against which all subsequent changes should be measured with any deviation being seen as decline. In reality the rate of construction was unsustainable once imperial funding was removed. Indeed the original plan for the Severan complex seems to have called for two *fora* articulated around the basilica and that the plan for the second *fora* was dropped on Caracalla's death, after the land earmarked for the development had already been levelled (Ward-Perkins 1993: 107). This abandonment can be seen in the same light as the failure to complete Thysdrus' amphitheatre.

The financial exertions that the Lepcitanian elite were exposed to by the production of the Severan complex and their reciprocal gestures in erecting statues to the imperial family may well have been exacerbated by the financial pressures that came with the 'gift' of oil from the city to Rome from Severus onwards (Mattingly 1988b: 35; *SHA*, *Severus*, 18.3, 23.2; Wilson is perhaps too optimistic as viewing this as a true gift 2007: 306–7). Additionally, Mattingly argues that the end of the Severan era saw the estates of three major families lose their financial link with the city as the estates of the Severans and those confiscated from executed Lepcitani, Plautianus under Severus and Lucius Septimius Aper under Caracalla, rolled into the estate of the Severii's successors (Mattingly 1988b: 36). If Mattingly is correct then the profits from significant lands within the city's territory would henceforth have not been available for the maintenance of the urban area and would, instead, have gone into imperial coffers. The reduction of the economic base, coupled with the gift and the draining nature of the new complex, would have undermined the elite's capacity to continue building. Over the long term they might have been able to retrench but as the next chapter will demonstrate the city's troubles were not over.

Sabratha's economy may have been struggling in the third century. Dore has suggested that a lack of building work in the later second and third centuries and the abandonment of building work in the East Forum Temple might demonstrate a reduction in the size of the city's economy (Dore 1988: 74, 84). Additionally the open-air sanctuary to the east of the city, which was likely dedicated to Saturn and Caelestis, was first abandoned and then turned into a burial ground in the course of the third century (Brouquier-Reddé 1992: 29; Kenrick 1986, Dore 1988: 74). Again, it must be noted that changes in public munificence can be attributed to several different processes. The failure to finish the work in the East Forum Temple or the abandonment of Saturn and Caelestis' sanctuary may say more about changes in religious adherence or the way that individuals related to the divine than economic problems; we have already seen changes to Saturn cult that were not linked to the economy. Dore suggests that Sabratha's inability to continue building new large-scale monuments from the later second century onwards, which is even more marked when compared to Severan Lepcis, may be due to a weaker agricultural potential than Lepcis (Dore 1988: 84). It may be that Sabratha had a smaller financial base than Lepcis, certainly the urban area was smaller, and that its own second-century building campaigns had overstretched the city but this argument also presupposes that Lepcis' Severan era building campaign was in some way normal; we should not judge other cities by Lepcis' lavish, imperially sponsored, scale of construction.

Crisis?

The 50 years between the Severan era and the reforms of Diocletian are often viewed as a period of crisis and in some way transitional between the 'high' imperial era and the 'later' Roman Empire. Such a viewpoint ignores continued monumentalisation and commemoration of building by inscriptions at even quite minor settlements in the later third century. That is not to say that there were no changes in the course of the period, certainly commemoration by inscription was not as fashionable, or perhaps as necessary, in 260 as it had been in 200, but we have seen that inscriptions were a key element of memorialising the imperially sponsored wall circuits of eastern Numidia and western Mauretania. It would be wrong, however, to view the decline in the attested rate of construction as a slackening of African provincials' taste for Roman culture. There was continued maintenance and beautification of domestic structures in many cities and, although at a lower level than in the Severan era, there was continued building and reconstruction of temples, baths and other structures as well as the continued dedication of altars and statues to gods and emperors. In addition to building in established cities the new *castella* of Numidia and Mauretania could be interpreted as new proto-urbanisation in that region, although much more archaeological work needs to be done to see what was there before Rome, and what was there after fortification, to come to definitive conclusions about these 'settlements'. Despite the limitations of the archaeological evidence, the third century also marks the almost imperceptible beginning of the transition from traditional urban religions to a Christianised or part-Christianised urban topography, an issue that will be a particular concern of the next chapter. The lack of material evidence for Christian activity shows that, despite the trouble it caused the Roman authorities, it was essentially still unimportant to the workings of the African city of the third century.

7

The Late Roman City:
Continuity & Christianisation

The 'D' Word

The late third-, fourth- and fifth-century city has sometimes been treated as an
unwelcome appendage to the glories of previous eras. Some classical historians and
archaeologists have avoided it, as the late Roman period seems a strange and alien place,
a time when old assumptions about society and religious expression were abandoned
by large sections of the Roman populace. In reality many of the changes in Roman
cities generally, and African cities particularly, can be traced back to earlier eras.

   Much academic ink has been spilled over the use of 'decline' to describe the state
of Roman cities and culture more generally in the third to fifth centuries, with considerable effort expended to find the moment when the rot set in and the Empire
began to fall. The late Roman city has been regarded as being very different from the
second-century city. Famously, Gibbon portrayed a world of increased adherence to
Christianity and other mystery religions as demonstrating a fall from the religious
sobriety of the classical age; intellectual rigour and philosophy had been replaced by
unnatural piety (Gibbon 1776–88). From the 1960s onwards the vibrancy of the post-
classical age and continuities with the past were stressed (e.g. Brown 1971), although,
in recent years, some scholars have again sought to emphasise material decline from
the heights of the Roman Empire (e.g. Ward-Perkins 2005). I do not wish to particularly engage with these arguments here except to point out that some of the debate
is subjective. Clearly the second century saw vast sums spent on the monumentalisation of the cities but this conspicuous consumption may in itself be responsible
for a reduction in building work in subsequent centuries; the smaller scale of much
later work can be seen as a necessary corrective, a return to sensible levels of spending. The fourth and fifth centuries saw several long-term processes at work in the
urban landscape, including alteration and maintenance of the urban heritage and, in

some cases, Christianisation of the built environment. These alterations, even if they sully the classical splendour of the earlier city, are not necessarily manifestations of decline; when, for example, streets were partially blocked or a forum invaded by private dwelling places or large, beautifully decorated houses were divided into smaller houses and artisanal installations, the city was being reframed in a useful way for its inhabitants' economic and social needs. These were the people who the urban framework served, not nineteenth- and twentieth-century historians whose ideal inviolate city was that of the Antonine and Severan eras (for a fuller treatment see: Sears 2007). As with the periods examined thus far, there cannot be a monolithic one size fits all approach for all cities. Even neighbouring cities could have quite discrepant experiences depending on a whole raft of economic, cultural and religious factors, not to mention the vagaries of chance.

Carthage: A Late Imperial Regional Capital

Many aspects of earlier euergetism and types of construction continued well into the fourth century in a wide range of African cities. Carthage was recognised as the second biggest city in the western Roman Empire and it remained the region's pre-eminent city beyond the Vandal conquest of 429 to 439 (e.g. Ausonius, *The Order of Famous Cities*, 2, 3; Fig. 7.1). Carthage was also the residence of many provincial and regional officials, paid by the Roman state, who needed substantial governmental buildings in which to work but who also provided the impetus for the maintenance and embellishment of the city and the provision of entertainment. Given these factors it should not be a surprise that the city experienced continuous improvements throughout the fourth century and into the Vandal period, with older buildings being renewed or turned over to new uses.

The fourth century did not begin well for Carthage. Between 306 and 324 the Empire was torn by a series of struggles for supremacy between rival emperors following the breakdown of the tetrarchy and in 308 the *vicarius* (vicar) of Africa, Domitius Alexander, set himself up as emperor in the city but was suppressed by 311 by his rival Maxentius. As in 238, the African elite were punished for supporting a usurper. Carthage and Cirta, Numidia's capital, were ravaged by his soldiers; as many as 6,000 were said to have died (Aurelius Victor, *On the Caesars*, 40; Zosimus, *New History*, 2.14.3–4). Maxentius was certainly hated enough in the region for Constantine I to court popularity by dispatching Maxentius' head there for public display following his death at the battle of Rome's Milvian Bridge in 312. Archaeologically it is difficult to assess the accuracy of the written texts. An inscription, erected in 324 by the proconsul, Maecilius Hilarianus, claimed that Constantine had universally improved buildings at the city with the word *conditor*, founder, being associated with his name; officially, at least, Constantine was to be seen as repairing the damage done to Carthage on a lavish scale, although there is a lack of archaeological evidence we can use to assess the text's veracity (*CIL*, 8.12524). A similar statement was made at

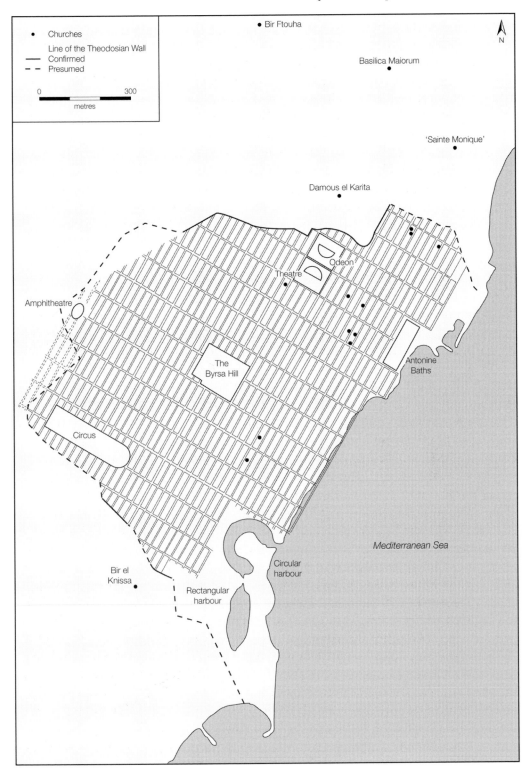

Fig. 7.1 Late Roman Carthage: after Ennabli 1997: 6.

Cirta, which was re-named Constantine to emphasise the emperor's role as its new founder. Six statues dedicated to the emperor are known from Cirta, along with a statue to his eldest son, Crispus, dedicated by a group that designated themselves as the *Constantinianenses* (the people of Constantine) (*ILAlg.*, 2.533, 581–2, 584–6; Lepelley 1981: 389–90). Constantine's positive attitude towards Cirta-Constantine is supported by a letter to a group of Numidian bishops that demonstrates that not only had he built one church at the city, he subsequently had the custom house converted into another church (*Letter of Constantine to the Numidian Bishops*).

Whatever the truth about Maxentian destruction, fourth-century Carthage was a growing city; for instance, an area on the city's north-east fringe was established in the early fourth century and despite, or potentially because of, Maxentius' depredations many large houses continued to be built, repaired and embellished well into the century (Anselmino 1992: 127–8; Stevens 1996: 196, 198–200). Some of Carthage's most important domestic mosaics date from this period and their content demonstrates the concerns and interests of their owners, both their rural land-holdings and their leisure pursuits frequently appear. For example, a famous mosaic in the House of the Master Julius depicts a turreted, aristocratic rural fortress containing a bath house and surrounded by its land-holdings, where peasants harvest and the aristocrat hunts; the House of the Greek Charioteers has a circus themed mosaic dated to the fourth century; and from the Carthaginian region of Dermech comes another fourth-century hunt mosaic (Dunbabin 1978: 53; Lepelley 1981: 12).

Mosaics are not alone in demonstrating the continued popularity of Carthage's entertainment venues in the fourth century. Augustine's *Confessions* documents his own pre-clerical, poetic performances in the theatre whilst the amphitheatre was clearly still in use when Symmachus, one of the great Roman aristocrats of the later fourth century, erected statues there as proconsul of Africa in 373–374 (August., *Conf.*, 4.2.3; *CIL*, 8.24584). Symmachus' gift obviously indicates that the amphitheatre was still in use but also that it was a place that the powerful could utilise to demonstrate their own personal munificence to contemporaries and future generations. The most pungent criticism of the Carthaginian attitude to the games came from the Gallic writer Salvian, who claimed that the Carthaginian populace was too busy attending the games to defend the city from the Vandals in 439, although this may be no more than a literary fiction designed to bolster his argument that the Roman Empire was collapsing because of its inhabitants' wickedness (Salvian, *Gub. Dei.*, 6.12). Salvian would presumably have been delighted if he had known that the theatre and the odeon (the venue for music recitals) were destroyed by the Vandals to prevent them being used as bases for resistance (Victor of Vita, *History of the Vandal Persecution*, 1.47).

The circus with its horse and chariot racing, the *ludi circenses*, was the most popular of all late Roman entertainments and Carthage provides a range of different archaeological evidence for this popularity. One of the most intriguing sets of circus-themed mosaics comes from a large complex from near the hill of Juno, where hunting scenes and representations of the gods were complemented by mosaics of horses and their riders. The primary colour of the horses' collars and the clothing of the individuals is blue, which Picard has suggested could either be due to the horse's owner being a fanatical 'blue' team fan or the structure being a club house for blue fans or riders (Picard 1964: 114). Either interpretation is possible but it is also possible that the blue colour scheme matched the horse owner's tastes.

Defixiones (curse tablets), found buried in graves near the circus where the spirits of the departed could be evoked to undermine the dedicant's enemies, also point to the popularity of charioteering in the late Empire and the desire to use supernatural agencies to affect race results. Dating from the third century at the earliest, the tablets contain spells designed to bind charioteers and horses from specific teams (Jordan 1988: 117–34); for instance tablet *CIL*, 8.12,508 was designed to bind horses from the red and blue teams to prevent them running properly (Gager 1992: 60–2). The tablets also indicate that the inhabitants of Carthage had access to the specialist Greek and magical knowledge necessary to produce the tablets (Rives 1997: 194–203).

Entertainment structures were not the only public monuments maintained in the city into the fourth century: inscriptions attest to baths, a temple of the eastern deities Cybele and Attis, and reservoirs, all being repaired (*CIL*, 8.24,582; *ILTun.*, 1093; *AE* 1949: 28 and 1955: 55; Lepelley 1981: 14–6). Just as importantly, statues to the reigning emperor continued to be erected throughout the period in order to express loyalty to Rome. As we have seen, bathing was a key part of the urban experience and many bath complexes were maintained into late antiquity. The city's Antonine Baths were working, apparently at full capacity, into the fifth century and would have remained a major focus of Carthaginian social life (Clover 1982: 9; Lezine et al. 1956: 426–8; Fig. 7.2). Many smaller establishments also seem to have been thriving; just one illustration of this is the small set of baths to the north of the Byrsa which were probably at their largest in the late fourth century (see Gerner Hansen 2002: 116–7). The Zaghouan aqueduct and its associated cisterns, which were key to the proper

Fig: 7.2 Antonine Baths.

functioning of the baths, were kept working into the Vandal period (Procopius, *Vandal War*, 2.1.2; Wilson 1998: 93).

Carthage in all eras was intrinsically connected with the Mediterranean trade routes and it remained a hub for the transit of goods and agricultural produce between the interior of Africa and the rest of the Empire, with all the through-put of money and investment in infrastructure at the city that such trade entailed. Its ports were crucial to this success and it is not surprising that work was ongoing on the city's commercial installations throughout antiquity. The mid- to late fourth century seems to have seen the construction or reconstruction of large warehouses around the rectangular harbour, the most likely explanation is that they were used to store agricultural produce before it was shipped overseas (Eadie & Humphrey 1977: 12). The importance of the trade to Rome is further graphically illustrated by the discovery of *ostraca* recording quantities of olive oil being shipped (Peña 1998). These quantities seem to be part of the *annona*, the tax in kind. The find on the admiralty island in the circular harbour, dated to 373–374, is as much an indication of the functioning of the late Roman state as it is a demonstration of trade vitality (Peña 1998). Trade piggy-backed on the flow of taxed goods but the state's interest was in taxation rather than a need to know how trade was performing. The continued functioning of Carthage's infrastructure is also demonstrated by an incomplete inscription listing ferry tariffs in the late antique coin, the *follis*, found near the *stagnum* (the modern Lac de Tunis). The inscription lists different prices for different passenger types, so a horseman paid four *folles*, a foot passenger paid one *follis* and a camel driver with a camel paid five (*CIL*, 8.24512).

The largest monument of late Roman Carthage was its wall circuit of 9.5km, constructed in 425 on the orders of Theodosius II (*Gallic Chronicle*, 98). Carthage's walls can be linked to Theodosius' provision of massive fortifications for Constantinople during his reign. By the fifth century most important cities had impressive enceintes, as much for the status they gave as for their defensive properties (Carthage's walls ultimately proved useless in warding off the Vandals but Constantinople's circuit kept out invaders until 1204), and Theodosius may have wished to give Carthage the monument to match its status. The psychological effect of the monument in terms of civic pride cannot be underestimated but they did have a negative impact on some areas of the urban fabric. The wall's construction led to houses that were in the way, some of which were only built in the fourth century, being destroyed and the withering of previously thriving urban areas which were now cut off from the rest of the city (Wells 1992: 118; Dietz 1992: 147; Eadie & Humphrey 1977: 16). The walls changed the nature of the city. Whilst it is in keeping with the Roman tradition of awarding important cities the right to build them as a reward, it goes against a Romano-African tradition of open cities. Many cities either never built walls or let their circuits decay over time. At Thamugadi, for instance, the colony's wall circuit, built in AD 100, was subsequently knocked down and houses constructed over the wall line (Ballu 1903: 89; Laurence et al. 2011; Sears 2007: 40–1, 84–5). The wall construction might have run counter to what some African populations had thought about wall circuits as

Map 5 Late Roman provinces.

definers of civic status, but it is impossible to know if that pertained to Carthage's elite; the text does not say if Theodosius' permission followed a Carthaginian request or whether it was a true external imposition of imperial will, so it is impossible to make definitive statements about the motivation behind their construction.

Carthage demonstrates some continuity in the function of its entertainment structures, its economy, its growth and in its general scale and complexity but, at the same time, the Theodosian Wall's construction marks a profound development in the city's urban topography (Stevens 1996: 198–200). The city's evolution was not a linear progression from its Roman origins through a period of expansion and monumentalisation and decline in the fourth and fifth centuries, not least because of the problems of defining 'improvement' and 'decline'. Instead we see an ongoing process of change across almost five centuries of Roman Carthage.

A Provincial Capital

Even in the later Roman Empire cities were still being moulded to conform to their inhabitants' views about the buildings they should contain. Under the emperors of the tetrarchy (285–305) and their successors the Empire's provinces were divided into smaller units to create greater efficiency and to limit the potential for a governor or army commander to rebel and set themselves up as an emperor due to the reduced resources that they controlled. By 313 Africa Proconsularis was divided into Proconsularis, Byzacena and Tripolitania and eastern Mauretania Caesarensis was hived off into a new province called Mauretania Sitifensis. Sitifis (see Chapters 2 and 5; Map 5; Fig. 7.3) became Sitifensis' provincial capital and building campaigns were launched to complement the existing urban infrastructure of at least two rich baths and a major temple (Mohamedi et al. 1991: 28–55; Sears 2007: 63–6).

The city's aristocracy were still building into the late Empire with a group of them paying for the temple to the Great Mother Cybele in 288 (Lepelley 1981: 498; *CIL*,

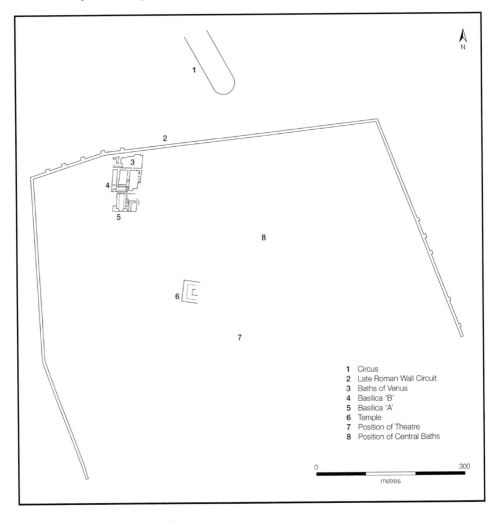

Fig. 7.3 Sitifis: after Février 1964: Fig. 14.

8.8457). However the scale of most of the building suggests that it is the product of the imperial authorities. Apparently, by 297–298, an amphitheatre had been built, although it is always possible that the dedicating inscription was actually for a repair or alteration masquerading as an entirely new structure; it was restored during the reign of Julian (361–363) (Gsell 1901: 201; Lepelley 1981: 499; *AE* 1928: 39 and *CIL*, 8.8482). As at Carthage, Sitifis' most impressive and perhaps costly late imperial monument is the wall circuit constructed in the second half of the fourth century. The rampart was around 5km long with towers constructed every 30m along the outside of the structure; it would have made a very definitive statement about the strength and enduring nature of Roman rule to the resident population, travellers and tribesmen who might consider revolting or raiding Roman territory (Février 1964: 683; Lepelley 1981: 498). During the fourth century the theatre was reconstructed and a circus built, whilst a late imperial inscription records the reconstruction of the governor's palace's porticoes; its construction surely dates to shortly after the provincial reorganisation (Gsell 1901: 200; Lepelley 1981: 501; Humphrey 1986: 314; Jouffroy 1986: 303; *AE* 1930: 46). Finally the city's *curator* (an official who was supposed to look after the urban fabric) and the city paid for the restoration of the bakeries and other building associated with the *annona* (*CIL*, 8.8480).

The late fourth century also saw the expansion of Sitifis' urban area. The northwest quarter of the town, just inside the city wall, developed substantially during the third quarter of the century when a new, clearly centrally planned, road grid was laid out and housing constructed (Février 1964: 682). Shops, a set of baths including a mosaic depicting Venus, and two Christian basilicas at right angles to each other, dated by epitaphs to pre-378 and pre-389, were also built in the new quarter (Février 1964: 679; Fentress 1990: 123; Gui et al. 1992: 84).

There is no explicit evidence that any of the work at Sitifis was connected to the new provincial organisation but the scale and nature of the building campaign is highly suggestive of a specific ideology of urban living being imposed on the city. For the imperial administration walls, a full set of entertainment facilities, baths and a governor's palace were not optional and to bring the city up to the requisite level it was necessary for a major scheme of improvement to be put into place. The change in role of the city may also have led to population increase through immigration or economic development that resulted in the need for the new regularly planned district.

Sitifis' prosperity must have been at least partly built on the salaries of imperial officials who resided there as well as the rich agricultural potential of the region (but see Chapter 2). This prosperity seems, in part, to have been interrupted by an earthquake in the early fifth century, before 419, which did considerable damage to the city and led to the all too familiar sight to a modern TV audience of the inhabitants camping out in the countryside for five days, presumably because they feared building collapse and aftershocks (August., *Serm.*, 19.6). Archaeological evidence for the earthquake is not overwhelming but it seems likely that it destroyed one of the Severan era baths, which were quickly rebuilt, albeit on a much reduced scale (Fentress 1989: 321–37; Mohamedi, et al. 1991: 39). The people of Sitifis may not have had the resources or perhaps desire to rebuild the baths to their Severan era size but the correct functioning of the city, the need to create properly washed Roman citizens, could not be ignored.

Continuities & Developments

Many other African cities maintained their urban fabric across the fourth century mirroring Carthage's continued wealth and development. Compared to the second century there is an obvious reduction in the construction of new entertainment and governmental structures and instead the authorities and individuals concentrated on maintaining the existing urban infrastructure; a difficult task given the multiplication of facilities such as baths and temples. That is not to say that all new, large-scale

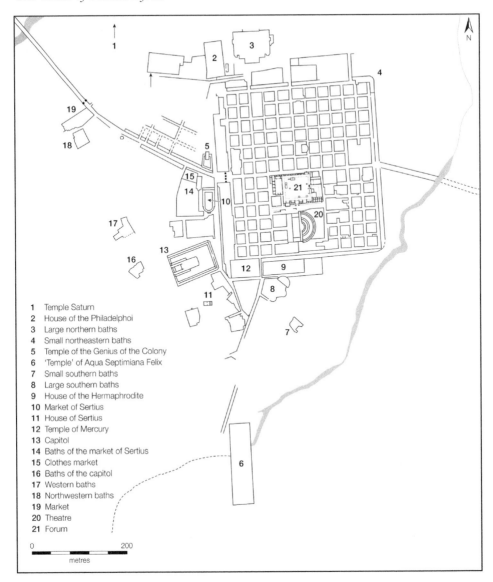

Fig. 7.4 Thamugadi: after Ballu 1911.

1 Temple Saturn
2 House of the Philadelphoi
3 Large northern baths
4 Small northeastern baths
5 Temple of the Genius of the Colony
6 'Temple' of Aqua Septimiana Felix
7 Small southern baths
8 Large southern baths
9 House of the Hermaphrodite
10 Market of Sertius
11 House of Sertius
12 Temple of Mercury
13 Capitol
14 Baths of the market of Sertius
15 Clothes market
16 Baths of the capitol
17 Western baths
18 Northwestern baths
19 Market
20 Theatre
21 Forum

building ceased but it was in the arena of church building that communities concentrated such efforts (see below).

Many cities' surface area, and presumably therefore their populations, were still expanding in the third and fourth centuries. The dating for these expansions is rarely exact both due to the problems of excavation established above (Introduction) and because individual monuments within these urban zones or at their peripheries are used as indicators of a district's age. Without precise excavation of the monuments and their surroundings the relationship between city district and monument will not be secure and dating city expansion enters the realm of educated guesswork.

Examples of this problem can be seen at a number of cities. At Thamugadi the arches on the roads from Lambaesis and Mascula have been taken to show that the city had spread rapidly by the reign of Marcus Aurelius (Fig. 7.4), whilst at Sufetula the arch of Diocletian to the south-west of the old city grid has been used to date the suburb to the third century (Ballu 1897: 111; 1911: 10–3; Février 1982a: 354; Duval 1982a: 614–5; Fig. 7.5). A final problematic case can be seen at Cuicul where a large quarter gradually formed to the south of the original *colonia* (Fig. 7.6). The area is framed to its north by the Severan forum and to the south by the second-century baths of Commodus and a late fourth- to early fifth-century episcopal complex. Février posed the question in 1964 as to whether or not the baths were placed into a land-scape devoid of public and private building and the question is not really answered except to say that there was at least building on the site of the 'house' of Bacchus from the second century onwards; we might suggest that it may have been a suburban area that was not fully built up until the fourth or fifth centuries (Février 1964: 10).

As we have already seen, entertainments were an important part of Romano-African culture so it should not be a surprise that city populations continued to maintain these structures into the fourth century and beyond. One indication of their importance is demonstrated by the inscriptions; there are more inscriptions recording public baths reconstruction or construction than for any other type of structure in the late Roman period. It was important not just to maintain the structure but also to record that maintenance had been done. Archaeological evidence also demonstrates ongoing maintenance of these structures and small public bath houses being constructed in many cities. To take Thugga as an example, the atrium of the central 'Licinian' Baths was refurbished between 367 and 383 and the baths of Aïn Doura to the south of the city were enlarged during the fourth century (*ILTun.*, 1500; Lepelley 1981: 221; Thébert 2003: 175). On the other hand, few new large bath complexes were constructed. The 'unfinished' baths at Lepcis Magna, which seem to date to the fourth century, are the largest set at around 1500m square, but even they were not entirely new, as half of the baths date to the second century AD (Goodchild 1965). In any case, the new portions of the baths were never completed; the population was unable to support the project. Given the expense of maintaining a structure such as the Hadrianic Baths this should not be surprising; what is interesting is that someone (the builder is unknown) thought that there should be a new set of baths at all. The idea of benefaction and urban improvement was present until the end of Roman Africa.

Alongside the maintenance of public entertainment facilities many aristocrats were constructing their own domestic bath suites; the houses of Europa, the Donkey and Castorius at Cuicul are a perfect example of this process. How private these baths were and what they say about bathing culture at the city is a matter for debate and cannot be answered conclusively (Thébert 2003: 482; Sears 2007: 86–8; Leone 2007: 57–9). The baths may demonstrate the city's elite creating private havens where they could continue traditional Roman cultural practices and entertain their friends and clients out of the public gaze, which could be seen as a movement away from traditional public bathing practices to a more privileged sequestered existence for elites (Blanchard-Lemée 1984: 29–32, 58–9, 85–100, 140–51, 161–6; Allais 1939: 35–44). However, the baths of the House of Europa had entrances into the house and the street which might imply a wider clientele than just the family and their guests. Whatever the motivation these 'private' suites and the maintenance of public baths demonstrate a continued commitment to bathing as a marker of proper cultured behaviour for urban populations.

Inscriptions referring to work on 'leisure' buildings (no inscriptions refer to circuses)

Date	Baths	Theatres	Amphitheatres
284–305	5	3	1
305–313	0	0	0
313–337	4	0	0
337–363	5	2	1
363–378	8	2	0
378–395	6	1	0
395–450	4	1	0

As this table shows, other types of entertainment facility were less likely to be repaired or constructed in the third to fifth centuries than baths were; although this may in part be due to small baths being less expensive than a circus and that there were fewer theatres, amphitheatres and circuses than baths to be repaired in any case. It was a rare city that built a second amphitheatre at any period. To take amphitheatres as an example, despite the lack of evidence for construction or reconstruction (both precisely dated works on an amphitheatre come from Sitifis), there is evidence to show that amphitheatres were still in use into the later Empire at a number of cities. We have already seen the continued functionality of Carthage's amphitheatre and there is evidence for the continued use of the amphitheatre at Theveste (Lequément 1967: 120), but perhaps the most striking evidence for the use of an amphitheatre in the late Empire is at the Civitatem Turbitanam.

According to their passion, saints Maxima, Donatilla and Secunda were executed there by the sword after a bear refused to harm them under the tetrarchs on 30 July 304 (most probably) for refusing to apostatise (Tilley 1996: 13–4). The women were subsequently buried in the place for condemned criminals next to the structure (*The Passion of Saints Maxima, Donatilla and Secunda*, 6). Depending on how much historicity one is prepared to concede to the account either the amphitheatre was in use in the early fourth century in a meaningful enough way to make it the obvious choice

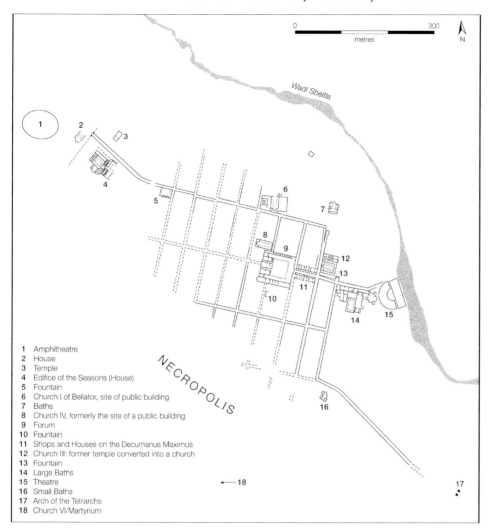

1 Amphitheatre
2 House
3 Temple
4 Edifice of the Seasons (House)
5 Fountain
6 Church I of Bellator, site of public building
7 Baths
8 Church IV, formerly the site of a public building
9 Forum
10 Fountain
11 Shops and Houses on the Decumanus Maximus
12 Church III: former temple converted into a church
13 Fountain
14 Large Baths
15 Theatre
16 Small Baths
17 Arch of the Tetrarchs
18 Church VI/Martyrium

Fig. 7.5 Sufetula: after Duval 1982a: Fig. 2.

for the punishment of dangerous violators of imperial law or the compiler or creator of the story, sometime in the fourth or fifth century, thought it likely that an amphitheatre could have been used during the Great Persecution as a venue for public execution. Civitatem Turbitanem's location is unclear but it was presumably either Thuburbo Maius or Thuburbo Minus. The fact that the former has an amphitheatre containing dedications to Constantine II (337–340) and a late antique Christian shrine gives some, admittedly inconclusive, weight to it being the passion's location. The presence of a Christian shrine in an amphitheatre was not unique to Thuburbo Maius, for instance the amphitheatre at Salona in Dalmatia had a similar structure. Their presence suggests that the amphitheatre was a potent symbol of persecution for Christians in late antiquity and in consequence they wished to spiritually and physically dominate the edifice (Dyggve 1951: 11; Bomgardner 2000: 198).

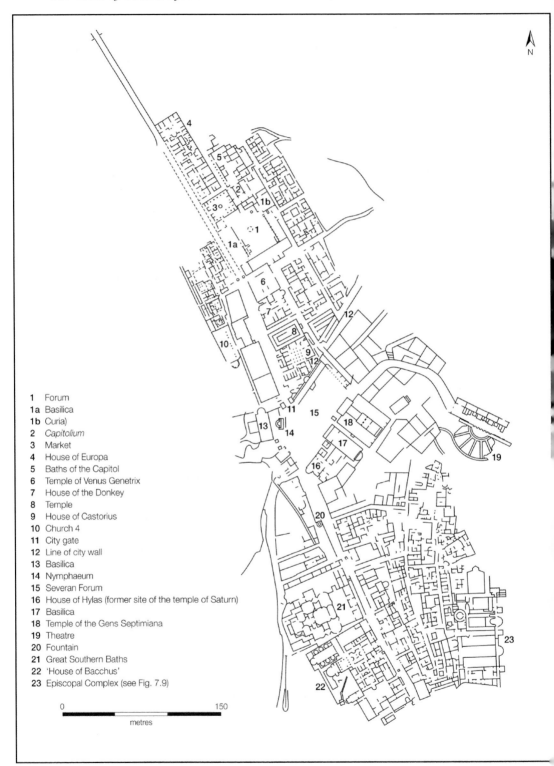

1   Forum
1a   Basilica
1b   Curia)
2   *Capitolium*
3   Market
4   House of Europa
5   Baths of the Capitol
6   Temple of Venus Genetrix
7   House of the Donkey
8   Temple
9   House of Castorius
10   Church 4
11   City gate
12   Line of city wall
13   Basilica
14   Nymphaeum
15   Severan Forum
16   House of Hylas (former site of the temple of Saturn)
17   Basilica
18   Temple of the Gens Septimiana
19   Theatre
20   Fountain
21   Great Southern Baths
22   'House of Bacchus'
23   Episcopal Complex (see Fig. 7.9)

0   150
                metres

Fig. 7.6 Cuicul: after Février 1968: 21a and Février 1964: Fig. 11.

The scale of work on baths compared to amphitheatres could reflect a change of priorities within urban populations, with a greater concentration on bathing than, for instance, gladiatorial combat. This could theoretically reflect Christian attitudes to bloodshed but such an impact on society is very difficult to pin down. Certainly Augustine's sermons, and before him Tertullian's works, are littered with invective condemning those who attended the shows and who took part in unholy activities such as chariot-racing, acting and gladiatorial combat (e.g. August., *En. in Ps.*, 81.16, 86.15, 94.15, 100.9, 147.19, 149.7; Tert. *On the Spectacles*; *Apology*, 15.5; *To the Nations*, 1.10.47). Augustine's account of the mania for gladiatorial contests from which his friend Alypius suffered is one of the great depictions of the passion and bloodlust the sport engendered in the populace (August., *Conf.*, 7.6.13). The criticisms are frequently directed at other Christians who watched lewd theatrical performances or the slaughter of the amphitheatre; many Christians could not be enticed away from their charms, let alone non-Christians. Contrary to popular thinking, not even the first Christian emperor, Constantine I, banned the games. A law of the emperor in 325 commands that people who would usually be condemned to the amphitheatre be instead sent to the mines, but this cannot have been intended for universal application as games were held across the Empire for the rest of the century; indeed the very next law in the Theodosian Code mentions games at Rome in 357 (*CTh*, 15.12.1–2). Instead Wiedemann may well be correct that the law only had a local application either at Berytus, the city where the law was posted, or at a regional level, to make up the numbers in the mines (Wiedemann 1992: 157).

Different types of evidence produce slightly different pictures of the vitality of 'leisure' pursuits. Inscriptions and archaeology suggest that bathing was flourishing with no loss of popularity or commitment to maintain the infrastructure. Theatres too were reasonably frequently maintained but amphitheatres and circuses may have been suffering from a lack of attention, with some, for instance the amphitheatre at Lepcis Magna, going out of use (Di Vita 1990: 464–5). The literary material suggests that all types of 'leisure' activity were thriving in the cities as they had been from the second century onwards but it was produced by a small number of individuals who had experience of only a few cities; it may be that the picture of sporadic investment in structures other than baths is a better indication of upkeep than Augustine's worries about his congregation's immorality.

We have previously seen the cities of Africa becoming populated by statuary. In late antiquity they continued to be erected, although increasingly they were only put up to honour emperors or their representatives; local aristocrats were becoming less likely to be commemorated for their beneficence. For instance at Sicca Veneria, a town in the north of Proconsularis with a famous Temple of Venus, six statues from late antiquity (probably) are known: to Helena, the mother of Constantine I from the city *curator*; to Constantius II from the city; to Valentinian I from the *curator* and the *ordo* of the city; to a dignitary, possibly the patron of the province; to a man who had the status of a *clarissimus*, a senator, who was a patron and *curator* of the city; and possibly one to the restorer of Venus' cult statue who was also a patron and *curator* of the city (*CIL*, 8.1633, 16,258, 1636, 15,878, 15,883, 15,881). The list of persons is fairly typical for the late Empire: three members of the imperial house and three individuals who were all above the level of local dignitary.

Erecting statues to the emperors and thereby demonstrating loyalty was clearly still a priority for the decurions and the *curator* at Sicca and other cities. The erection of statues also linked the fourth-century populace to their ancestors; traditional activities and methods of commemoration, even if changing gradually over time, provided continuity and created a living museum that contributed to the collective memory of the town. Even with a focus on the emperors the inscribed base showed who had paid for the statues, which imperial official had dedicated them and the permission of the council for its siting; the rest of the population could look at the statues and read their bases. The statue still bound all levels of the Empire together: emperor; governor; city councillor; members of the aristocracy; general public. The focus of commemoration may have changed slightly but the statues provided a link to the past, a way for the wealthy to showcase themselves and an improved urban environment.

Cities in Trouble?

Not all cities were thriving. We have already seen Lepcis and Sabratha struggling in the third century, but if anything the Tripolitanian cities' problems worsened from the fourth century onwards as an earthquake and raids from the pre-desert by the Austoriani ravaged their lands and impacted on their economic base (Amm., 28.6.2–4; Mattingly 1995: 176–7; Sears 2007: 70–8, 84, 96). The last substantial set of building inscriptions at the two cities date from the 360s and 370s, with the last works being on a set of baths paid for by the governor, Flavius Vivius Benedictus, who was honoured in 378 by the *ordo* and the people in thanks for the work (*IRT*, 103). Alongside the failure to complete the 'unfinished baths' mentioned above, the suburban hunting baths were also abandoned (Goodchild 1965); the city clearly no longer had the finances to warrant the construction of new facilities in the later fourth century. The Tripolitanian cities were not alone in suffering from warfare. Problems with tribal groupings occurred in Mauretania during the later third and fourth centuries. That of the native tribal chief Firmus (372–375), a member of a family who repeatedly served as imperial officials both before and after his revolt, was said to have devastated Caesarea (Amm., 29.5.18–9).

Utica, the former capital of Roman Africa, may also have been struggling in late antiquity. An analysis of the results of excavation, inscriptions and mosaics suggests relatively limited maintenance work after the early fourth century, although it was still a city into the Byzantine period. The apparent relative lack of monumental building activity could reflect economic problems. Sitting at the head of the Bagradas valley, Utica had always been a major transit point for the export of African agricultural produce to Italy and it has been argued that the harbour had begun to silt up during the third century, restricting trade at Utica and correspondingly reducing the flow of money through the city (Lepelley 1981: 243). However, analysis on silt cores suggests that the silting up of the harbour post-dates the Roman period; other explanations for the apparent lack of building need to be sought (Chelbi et al. 1995).

The only indication of any large-scale repairs at Utica comes from around AD 324 when the proconsul, Maecilius Hilarianus, who we have already met at Carthage, dedicated a statue in honour of Constantine the Great (*CIL*, 8.1179). As with the contemporary inscription from Carthage, the base details the generosity and clemency of the emperor in ornamenting the city, suggesting work on public buildings made possible either by a grant of money or through the cancellation of taxes or debts. Had Utica also suffered from the vengeance of Maxentius? Possibly; we could alternatively interpret these inscriptions as the work an imperial official encouraging loyalty to the emperor and suggest that the words of renewal did not always reflect any concrete reality. However, the audience for the inscriptions, the Carthaginian and Utican elites and imperial officials, resident at or in transit through the city, were unlikely to be impressed by mere rhetoric and although we might be sceptical of such all-encompassing claims without concrete support from excavation, it is likely that major works were undertaken at Utica. So the lack of fourth-century building inscriptions may not mark the absence of building per se, but archaeologists' failure to recover them or the Utican elite's failure to commemorate building work through inscriptions.

Away from public building some churches seem to have been constructed but they have not been excavated so their date is unclear. Domestic housing though suggests significant changes at Utica with a series of houses showing improvements during the fourth century. For instance, the House of Love and Psyche is named after a late third-century or early fourth-century mosaic of those deities (Duliere 1974: 4). The House of the Hunt demonstrates considerable embellishment, with a new fourth-century peristyle courtyard. The colonnaded walkways around the courtyard were decorated with mosaic panels depicting hunting scenes, which can be dated to post-355–361 because of coins of Constantius II, found within the ground levelling layer beneath the mosaics (Alexander & Ennaifer 1973: 68). However other Utican houses had reached their apogee in the course of the second century and in the fourth century they were often split up, reduced in size and sometimes replaced by artisanal installations. This is not necessarily indicative of economic decline, however. A reduction in size need not mean a reduction in opulence as the reduced house could be made more luxurious than its earlier incarnations. The division of houses into multiple units could also be due to the owners wanting to realise some of the value of their property by renting or selling parts of their home for other uses. This process could be due to financial pressures among members of the elite and would therefore point to changes being driven by difficulties. Alternatively, it could simply indicate population growth leading to intensification of urban space. Finally the conversion of houses for artisanal uses could suggest economic growth.

Utica's experience in the fourth century then is far from clear; the apparent lack of continued monumental construction might suggest a contraction in the city or the elite's resources or a reduction in their willingness to fund such work. Alternatively the splitting up of houses and the creation of new workshops might suggest population and economic growth.

That some cities were suffering difficulties as others thrived should not be a surprise. No society demonstrates uniform linear growth or contraction for all its cities; as some cities draw trade, industry or political functions to them other cities might lose them. The Roman world was no different and it is essential the failures be set against the successes. The general pattern is of continued maintenance and improvement in urban areas across Africa.

New Euergetism, New Monuments

Perhaps the most eye-catching element of the changes that took place in the late Roman city was the destruction of elements of the pagan religious heritage and the Christianisation of the city (Fig. 7.7). Christianity became a legal religion in 313 and, apart from Julian's brief reign (361–363), it was the emperors' religion after Constantine I's removal of his last rival, Licinius, in 324. From that point onwards, imperial favour flowed to the churches and laws were passed inhibiting pagan religious practice and eventually closing the temples and banning paganism outright (*CTh.*, 16). This legislative process augmented a gradual organic process of personal conversion during the fourth and fifth centuries. As Christian beliefs grew in importance and became the Empire's dominant religious force, the cities were changed by Christians. As one God replaced a multiplicity of deities, so churches, baptisteries, bishops' palaces, monasteries and martyria (the tombs of martyrs) replaced temples and shrines. Changes in religious belief were echoed in the built environment.

Assessing the importance of the change in religious belief is complicated. On the one hand ancestral ways of understanding the divine and humanity's place in the world were entirely replaced. This was not just a question of cosmetic changes, such as giving the chief divinity a new name. The newly dominant faith had different concepts of how other faiths and imperial power should be treated to the established cults. Wielders of spiritual power, men and women, who had privileged access to God and the saints, could now successfully oppose emperors, the previous ultimate religious authority. On the other hand, the stark opposition between 'paganism' and Christianity as expressed in our literary sources, the clergy and 'pagan' aristocrats who were at the heart of theological debates between the faiths, are perhaps overstated; there may have been considerably more fluidity between religious communities and a more organic process of Christianisation than has sometimes been envisaged.

Late Roman Christianity was not a monolithic religion that encompassed all adherents within a unified system. There was clearly fluidity between sects and religions; individuals' understanding of what was correct Christian belief and practice varied. For instance, Augustine criticised the survival of pre-Christian activities in the Church, leading a not entirely successful campaign, along with Bishop Aurelius of Carthage, to stamp out feasting at martyrs' tombs and ritual dancing which reflected

Fig. 7.7 The remains of a church from the Dermech region of Carthage.

pagan feasts for the ancestors whilst Christians were perfectly comfortable with the practice (e.g. August., *Serm.*, 252; *Ep.*, 22, 29). On one occasion Augustine discovered that his congregation had, during his absence, baptised themselves in the sea following a pre-Christian tradition; the congregation were annoyed at the priests' charges of pagan behaviour because they claimed that no one had ever told them that such rites were pagan (e.g. August., *Ep.*, 23 and *Serm.*, 311.5; 196.4). Others who defined themselves as Christians ignored the clergy and also attended temples or made use of magic (e.g. August., *En. in Ps.*, 94.15, *Serm.*, 2.4; Salvian, *Gub. Dei.*, 8.2).

The extent of overlap between faiths can be seen in Augustine's acerbic comment that many Africans could not tell the difference between Saturn and the Christian God, perhaps, it is suggested, because of their all encompassing power, their intimate relationship with their adherents and, as God was presented in Africa at least, a stern love for man and a requirement that this love be reciprocated (August., *Cons. ev.*, 1.21.29–22.30; see Tertullian, *Scorpiace*, 6; Frend 1952: 97–103). Other individuals, who thought of themselves as Christians, continued to attend the temples alongside going to church, a situation that both Augustine and Salvian ranted about (Salvian,

Gub. Dei., 8.2; August., *Serm.*, 2.4 and *En. in Ps.*, 88). The two clergymen may have exaggerated the extent of the 'problem' to excoriate even more forcefully those who flirted with more than one religious system, but equally the religious boundary may not have appeared rigid, or even existed, for many. Indeed, Augustine's career demonstrates the extraordinary permeability of religious faith in Africa in this period. Starting out as a Catholic, he progressed to Manichaeism, adhered to philosophical schools coupled with an interest in astrology and then numerology; the latter obsession continued into his career as a Catholic priest and bishop following his famous conversion at Cassiacum in Italy in 386–387 (see August., *Conf.*, 3–9; *Serm.*, 264.5).

There was even more fluidity between Christian sects such as the Catholics and Donatists, whose divisions had emerged out of the Great Persecution under Diocletian. It is a complicated and much debated split, and the details cannot be discussed here because of the limitations of space, but essentially during the persecution some Christians lapsed and offered sacrifice to the gods rather than be killed, whilst others were martyred for their faith (see Frend 1952 or Sears 2007: 8–16). In the aftermath personality clashes and regional disputes led to various bishops being accused of collaborating with the pagan authorities and a split evolved with the Catholics pre-eminent in Proconsularis and the Donatists (who referred to themselves as Catholics) dominant in Numidia. Despite disagreements that occasionally led to violence, Augustine's texts demonstrate that Christians moved between the sects, attended each other's ceremonies and were often on good terms with individuals from other groups; indeed some of Augustine's relatives were Donatists (e.g. August., *Ep.*, 52, 66, 142). Our rigid definitions of sects and religions do not fit the multi-faceted late Roman world where personal definitions of legitimate religious behaviour could cut across the categories provided by religious authorities (see Rives 1995: 223–34 for an earlier period). The interplay between 'official' religion, whether traditional or Christian, and a multiplicity of practices affected how religion was built into the city in the later Roman Empire, but looking at the outcome – the buildings – does not tell us how the construction of these structures was actually negotiated.

The most obvious consequence of the change in religious adherence was a steady decline in the documented repair or construction of temples to the traditional gods throughout the fourth century (Sears 2007: 92–9). There are more examples known from the reign of Diocletian and the tetrarchy (285–305) than the rest of the fourth century combined; the last known example of temple repair, at Henchir Morabba, is dated to 383–395 (*CIL*, 8.23,968–9; Sears 2007: 92–3). This does not necessarily mean that repairs to temples simply stopped but if work was continuing those who paid for it increasingly found it impolitic to commemorate their generosity. Archaeological evidence for the continued use of temples into the late fourth and fifth centuries is scanty because of the destruction of late antique occupation layers by excavators keen to reveal original mosaic or marble floors or because of the ephemerality of the late antique levels. It is impossible to come to an informed statistical conclusion about the proportion of temples that were abandoned or destroyed in the course of the fourth century, but some general conclusions can be reached. Not all destruction was the handiwork of Christians. Some temples' destruction in the fourth century was due to fire, always common in pre-modern cities, the consequences of time or earthquake rather than the action of Christians. In such cases, however, temples may not have been repaired due to the impact of anti-pagan legislation, financial constraints or because the community no longer cared about the cult place. Examples of this can be seen to the east of our region in Cyrenaica. At Cyrene the sanctuary of Demeter and Persephone was largely abandoned as a religious site following an earthquake in 262 and a century later the earthquake of 365 partly destroyed the sanctuary of Apollo and the Temple of Zeus (White 1984: 93–103, 118–9; Goodchild et al. 1958: 39–41; Plate 29). Neither of these destructions were the consequence of Christian actions but both led to the abandonment of cult places.

The laws against using temples for pagan worship meant that African communities had to make choices about what to do with structures that their ancestors had lavished money on. Should they let them just collapse or reuse them, risking angering the gods? Increasingly the temples were put to new uses. The *capitolium* at Abthungi in Byzacena for instance became a meeting place for a *collegium*, while the basements of Thuburbo Maius' *capitolium* had artisanal installations inserted into them (*CIL*, 8.11,205 = 8.928; Alexander et al. 1980: xxiii, 76). A relatively common development was for monuments to become museums or art galleries for the city's statuary (Lepelley 1994). For example, the Temple of Apollo at Bulla Regia seems to have become a repository for statues moved from other temples in the city (Merlin 1908; Quoniam 1952: 466). At Caesarea, however, the population transferred statues from damaged or abandoned locations to a hall in the Great Western Baths. The statue of Hercules, for instance, was placed on a pedestal inscribed with four lines of text, the first on the front, 'HERCVLI', and the others on the side, 'TRANSLATA / DE SORDENTIBVS / LOCIS', 'Hercules. Moved from a decayed place' (*CIL*, 8.20,963; Lepelley 1994: 10–1). It is interesting that the sponsors of this movement thought it important not just to move the statue, which could have been due to civic pride or religious devotion, but to record that it had been moved. In doing so they provided the observer with the reminder that not only had the statue been moved but its previous location was decrepit. There were many potential responses for the literate observer to the text – e.g. pride at the city having maintained the statue or anxiety at urban decay – but the memory of urban change was definitively written into the built environment (see Thomas 2003: 139). The movement of the statues has been connected to the damage done to the city by Firmus but there is no actual evidence to connect the two episodes (Amm., 29.5.18); they could have come from abandoned temples. What we are seeing are monuments, often temples, which were judged as being surplus to requirements and recycled as part of a process of re-prioritising the urban fabric.

It can be very difficult to tell how long a temple had lain abandoned before it was reused if the reuse cleared away abandonment layers. It is also rare that the new structure has definitive datable foundation deposits. So, at Cuicul the site of the Temple of Frugifer (Saturn) had a basilica and the House of Hylas built over it in 364–367 (Le Glay 1966: 202–6; Blanchard-Lemée 1975: 172; Fig. 7.6). The stelae devoted to the god were spread over an area of around 200m in diameter as building material in houses, walls and as road paving (Allais 1953: 64; Le Glay 1966: 206–37). At Thamugadi stelae of Saturn were also spread over a wide area (1km or more), with some being re-employed in a wall around the *capitolium* (Le Glay 1966: 130–61). An even odder example comes from Mactar where a dedication to Apollo was reused as paving in the Temple of Apollo (*AE* 1983: 976). It is difficult to be certain what the implications of this are. Clearly the stelae were not treated as inviolable objects, but the exact date of their reuse and the reasons for the temples' abandonment are unclear. At Thamugadi one pagan god's sanctuary was despoiled but another was repaired with that material, demonstrating the problems of a simple 'Christians destroying pagan sanctuaries' narrative. The devotees of Apollo at Mactar could be said to be using one of their own offerings for the benefit of the god, presumably the dedication was treated with some reverence as it was reused. The Cuiculitanian use of stelae as paving does, however, suggest deliberate Christian triumphalism. The constant trampling of the stelae evoked the destruction of the deity's influence in the city and in the wider Empire. The Christians of Gaza in Palestine, for instance, had similar ideas using inscriptions from the Temple of Marnas to pave the entrance to their new church (Mark the Deacon, *Life of Porphyry of Gaza*, 75–6; Moralee 2006: 197–203). In Africa, an even more explicit example of Saturn's overthrow by Christ comes from Mascula, where one was used in a church's foundations (*CIL*, 8.17,676; Le Glay 1966: 167). Highlighting the general ineffectuality of the pagan gods may have helped to speed up the process of conversion through intimidation but also through the demonstration of the Christian God's superior spiritual power; after all if a deity could not protect their own sacred space how could they improve the lives of their devotees?

An alternative reading, in the light of Augustine's comments about syncretism, might be that the replacement of Saturn cult temples and the incorporation of Saturn stelae into the churches of Africa at places such as Mascula had less to do with blotting out the pagan past than incorporating previous religious expressions of the relationship between humanity and the 'Great God' into the built environment of the new conception of God (Le Glay 1966a: 301). However, whilst some within the Christian congregations might have had an open conception of man's relationship to supernatural power, it is unlikely that Christian clergy would have thought of Saturn and Christ being one and the same.

The full-blown conversion of temples into churches seems to have begun during the fourth century in Africa. Some of the conversions may have been designed to remind pagans of the new political reality of the Christian emperors or to aid conversion as discussed above. In some cases it may have more to do with reusing conveniently abandoned structures located in the heart of the urban area. These temple-church conversions are often very badly dated and it is impossible to create a detailed analysis of the phases of conversion and when it reached its height. Instead of coin or pottery evidence, stylistic comparisons of architectural decoration are used to provide a date, a method that can provide an indication of a broad range of years but which is also subjective.

Comparisons with other regions would suggest that the late fifth century would be the horizon when the process of temple to church conversion started in earnest, but in Africa it began in the late fourth to early fifth centuries, with the process continuing well into the Byzantine period (sixth–seventh century) (see Teichner 1996; Bayliss 2004; Sears 2007: 93–9). The competition for religious space (and adherents) between Donatist and Catholic Christians and the vitality of the cities preventing congregations erecting churches wherever they wanted could have started the process in Africa at an earlier date than elsewhere. Conversion could take many forms. Some temples were levelled to their foundations or their podium before a church was erected out of the *spolia* (material robbed out of earlier buildings) and new material. Others churches reused substantial elements of the previous temple. The fifth-century (probably) church in the *forum vetus* at Lepcis Magna, for instance, was placed on a former temple that had been stripped back to its podium (Goodchild & Ward-Perkins 1953; Plate 30). A colonnaded church with an apse and a portico that encroached on a pre-existing street was placed on the podium, introducing Christian cult into the heart of the town that had been dominated by temples since the public square was first constituted in the second century BC. The significance of such a change should not be ignored.

The temple building itself was only part of the sacred furniture of African cults. The cult statue representing the deity was crucial to the proper functioning of a cult. Their destruction was probably more shocking than the damage to gods' precincts. It is not easy to be certain with damaged statues what or who caused the damage. Statues with crosses carved on to them or with mutilated faces are likely to be the victims of Christian depredations but these are relatively rare; damage could occur through the ravages of time, earthquake and accidental fire. At Carthage one group of traditional believers clearly feared for the future of their cultic statues and believed that they should be protected. Excavations in the nineteenth century revealed a cache of statues, hidden in a sealed underground room near the cisterns of Bordj-Djedid; mosaics in the rooms above seem to have been created to hide the statues. Oil lamps decorated with Christian symbols indicated the rough period of the cache that included both marble and terracotta statues of deities such as Jupiter, Isis and Mithras (Gauckler 1899: 156–65). The cache also contained a famous inscription of a college of 12 priests and a *mater sacrorum* (mother of the sacred rites) who were in the service of the god Iupiter Hammon Barbarus Silvanus (*CIL*, 8.24,519; Le Glay 1966 2.308; Cadotte 2007: 529; Plate 31).

Although temple conversion is an eye-catching element of religious change, the vast majority of churches were not built over pagan sacred monuments; indeed many were built well away from the cities' *fora*. Built in the burial zones that ringed the cities, cemetery churches, which had their genesis in the Christian burial places that had been evolving from the third century onwards, were among those churches on the urban periphery (see Chapter 6). As we have seen, some Christian burial places were special, blessed by the presence of a saint or martyr and attracting other burials. By the fifth century burial *ad sanctos*, around the saints, was sought by some in the belief that spiritual reward would be gained in heaven because of physical proximity to the remains of the martyrs. This belief was contrary to official Christian theology and Augustine, when asked in about a specific case of a mother who wished to bury her son near a saint, confirmed that burial near a martyr was not going to benefit the soul of the deceased (August., *On the Care for the Dead*). Augustine, however, also advised that the mother be allowed to do as she wished given that she was, after all, recently bereaved. Practice and popular belief clearly could overrule official dogma in the fifth century. Belief and the funds available to Christian communities meant that cemetery churches were ripe for monumentalisation after the fourth century. At Carthage the Damous el-Karita is one of the most obvious examples of this monu-mentalising process. Built to the north of the city, the complex is huge (150+m by 65m) with atria, chapels, halls and the church itself (Plate 32; Fig. 7.8). Repaired and expanded into the Vandal and Byzantine periods, the church's interior was a veri-table forest of columns that would have restricted lines of site within the structure, limiting the mind's ability to grasp it all at once and increasing the sense of awe that the congregation would have felt in such a locus of spiritual power when they attended church. The structure can compete in its magnificence and size with most of the pre-Christian structures of the city. It may not be a coincidence that when the Theodosian wall was built, the road out to the Damous el-Karita was not closed off and was instead provided with a gate through the new circuit.

Cemetery churches were not the only basilicas constructed away from the civic centres of the cities. There could be various reasons for this. As we have already seen many African cities were still thriving or expanding in the late Roman period whilst their *fora* were functioning as centres of civic display. In such circumstances it may have been expensive to buy land and build a church, especially a large church, in the centre of a city; the periphery may have been more viable. There may also have been ideological reasons for ignoring the existing city centre, which were full of temples, and creating a Christian urban topography based around its own sacred space. We have seen the revulsion produced in some of the Christian community by the idols of the gods and the major Christian complexes at cities such as Theveste, Thamugadi, Sitifis, Sabratha and Cuicul might in part be a response to the existing non-Christian sacred topography (Figs 7.9 and 7.10). Certainly at Tipasa the writer of the *Passion of Saint Salsa*, and presumably his audience, conceived of part of the city as the *collis templensis*, the hill of the temples, which could be identified with the area around the forum and its associated temples (*Passion of St Salsa*, 3). The city's major churches, the cathedral and the basilica of Saint Salsa, built during the course of the fourth century, created alternative places of sacred power on the city's periphery, which in the case of the latter attracted pilgrims from across the region. Complexes like the basilica of Saint Salsa and the Damous el-Karita created sacred Christian zones around the city that provided foci for the Christian population and rivals to the great temple com-plexes of the past.

Some of the urban churches built in the course of the fifth century, and par-ticularly in Carthage, were vast and can be seen as replacements for the municipal

Fig. 7.8 The subterranean baptistery of the Damous el-Karita complex.

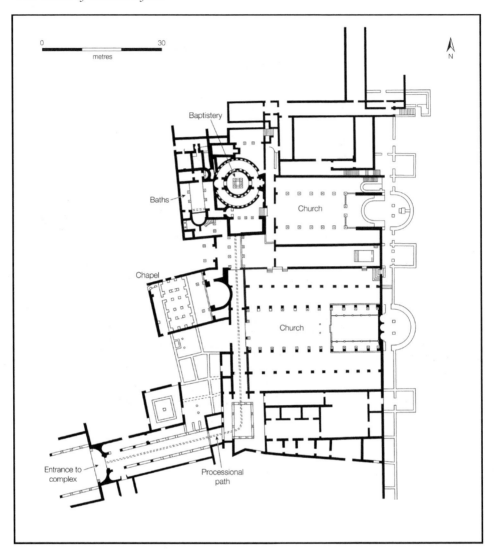

Fig. 7.9 Cuicul's Episcopal complex: after Février 1964: Fig. 8.

buildings of an earlier era. The multiplication of churches at other sites can be striking. For instance, the small settlement of Oued R'zel in southern Numidia was
provided with six separate churches between the fifth and seventh centuries. The
size, luxury (demonstrated by the use of marble, wall-paintings and mosaics) and
number of churches should not necessarily be seen as a marker of the number of
Christians at a city but, like the monuments of the classical city, are markers of the
ambitions and wealth of the community (Bowden 2001: 61). Like earlier monuments
they could be used to show the generosity of the elite justifying their great wealth
and domination over the town. For instance at Cuicul a group who, on the basis of
their names, may be connected to the town's aristocracy, paid for a mosaic paving in
the northern of the two churches in the episcopal complex (*CIL*, 8.8344–8; *AE* 1914:

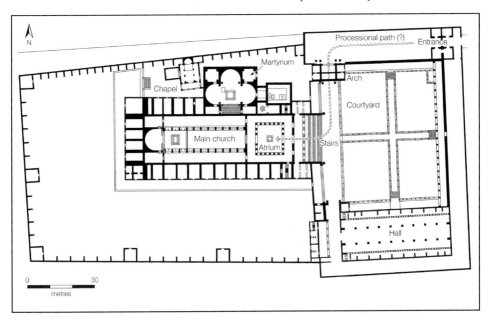

Fig. 7.10 Theveste's basilica: after De Roch, S. (1952) *Tébessa: antique Theveste*, Algiers. Fig. 1.

4–5; *BCTH*, 1914: 306; Lepelley 1981: 404, 411–2). However, the corporate nature of the Christian Church, which received donations from across its congregation, also provided an outlet for construction by the Christian population as a whole. All members of the church could feel that they were playing their role in the creation of a house of God; the psychological impact of this would be quite different from a focus on individual benefactors. Such a transformation in the production of a monumental urban environment may also have impacted upon the status of traditional elites and contributed to the growth in power of the bishops and clergy who controlled such community building. Another reason for the multiplication of churches in African cities was the need for all of the different sects to have their own places of worship. By the later fourth century it seems likely that most African cities had at least Catholic and Donatist churches but there were other schismatic groups, some of which would have had their own churches, although small groups might have met in houses (Optatus 3.4; August., *Haer.*, 86).

A Literary Corrective

We have already noted that we are often reliant on the literary evidence of a very few highly educated men for late Roman society. The agendas of these sources cause us problems due to their subjectivity and because they represent the views of only a small percentage of African society. Archaeological excavation, as we have seen, does not necessarily provide us with a corrective to these accounts due to the frequent lacunae in the evidence and the conduct of excavation until the mid-twentieth century. The picture provided by the archaeology is one of relatively little spending on temples and their increasingly frequent destruction and conversion for new uses in the late fourth and early fifth centuries. On the other hand Augustine's works, despite his hostility to paganism, provide occasional glimpses into a world where pagan religions remained popular and locally powerful. Two pertinent examples of pagan-Christian violence demonstrate both the physical impact of the increased power of Christianity and the reaction of pagan communities. The first occurred at Sufes in 399. A group of Christians had destroyed a statue of Hercules, understandably angering the god's adherents, who responded by murdering a number of Christians. Realising the danger they were in, the community wrote to Augustine begging him to intervene with the authorities to prevent their wrath falling on the city (August., *Ep.*, 50). Augustine sarcastically replied that he would restore the statue if the pagans revived the dead Christians. The anecdote demonstrates not only the vociferous anti-idolatry of some Christians but also the local strength of traditional believers; albeit they were scared about the consequences of their actions.

The second episode occurred at Calama (August., *Ep.*, 90–1, 103–4). In 408 a church was attacked, damaged and plundered and a Christian killed following an attempt by clergy to interrupt an illegal pagan procession in front of the church (August., *Ep.*, 91.8). The city authorities refused to intervene to uphold the law that prevented pagan rites taking place or to punish those who had attacked the churches or murdered the Christian, presumably because their sympathies did not lie with the Christians or because they were afraid to go against the cult's devotees. Nectarius, Augustine's pagan Calaman correspondent, feared that higher levels of provincial administration, more exposed to imperial views of Christian-pagan relations, would not take a lenient view of the killing and asked Augustine to intercede. Perhaps the Calaman violence could be linked with the rebuilding of the Temple of Apollo, the movement of a shrine to Victorious Fortune to a central position in the town and several building inscriptions at the city in the third and fourth centuries (*ILAlg.*, 1.250, 179, 255–6, 260, 288; Lepelley 1981: 91–2). The inscriptions suggest a clear desire to improve the religious and non-religious urban landscape and might therefore indicate a traditional conception of the world among the Calaman elite, and perhaps the wider community, who might react badly to Christian attempts to undermine their ritual practices.

It may be that the episodes at Sufes and Calama demonstrate that Christianity was not as powerful in the interior of the region as it was on the coast. However, Augustine's works demonstrate that even in Carthage, the centre of imperial administration in Africa, traditional religious practices and beliefs remained popular into the late fourth century. Elements of Augustine's account of the processions in honour of Caelestis that took place between 371 and 383 may or may not be tendentious, the parade of prostitutes (*meretricia pompa*) being the major point of dispute, but it is clear from his account that many people attended and enjoyed the rites and performances of 'lewd dancing' and 'obscene songs', which presumably had a fertility rite aspect to them (August., *De civ. dei*, 2.4 and 26; Rives 1994: 301–2).

The archaeological and literary evidence therefore provides a mixed picture of religious life in late Roman Africa. Official pagan cults were suppressed by the closure of temples and increasingly by Christian militancy that interrupted pagan processions, destroyed idols and converted churches for their own use. However, the evidence demonstrates the continued, if declining strength, of traditional religious observance and some individuals that incorporated practice from more than one religious system.

Continuity & Transformation

Late Roman Africa demonstrates both continuity and transformation from the early imperial period. Many cities were still constructing and repairing a range of building types that would not have looked out of place in the middle of the second century, demonstrating not only continued care for the appearance of the city but also for its functionality. The continued maintenance and construction of baths in particular demonstrates the vitality of ideals about cleanliness and socialising, as well as the cities' continued ability to marshal the funds and workmen to undertake the work. We should not overlook the fact that there was, however, a decrease in the number of traditional monuments being built in the fourth century. It should also be remembered that not all cities developed in the same way in the later Roman period and that local circumstances, as well as Mediterranean-wide social, political and economic factors, played a part in how well a city responded to the challenges of the century.

The gradual conversion of the population to Christianity was an ongoing factor within society during the fourth and early fifth centuries. This, of course, was a major religious change that had far-reaching consequences for African society and led to the construction of large numbers of new churches and associated structures. However, it would not be correct to regard the process of conversion as anywhere near complete at the time of the Vandal invasion, with a range of sources testifying to the continued worship of the old gods. Barton's statement that 'Before the end of the third century Africa seems to have been predominantly Christian, although paganism lingered on in a few places as late as the early fifth century' is conditioned by the agendas of our Christian-centric literary sources, destroyed temples and new churches and it fails to take into account the hints within the sources of considerable adherence to the old religions and the overlap in practices and beliefs (syncretism) between those who identified themselves as traditional believers and those who identified themselves as Christians (Barton 1972: 59). The construction of churches may have occupied much of the available funds in some late Roman cities, which may partly explain why other building types were less likely to be constructed or reconstructed than in previous eras. This should not be seen as a rejection of traditional Roman culture beyond its religion, and churches became an opportunity to demonstrate wealth via a new media.

8

Roman Africa?

Variety

This book has examined the evolution of the cities of Africa under Roman rule. What it remains to do is briefly consider what type of urban civilisation it produced. Roman Africa was clearly a diverse region ecologically, economically and cultur- ally, and this diversity had a profound effect upon the evolution and nature of cities and city life. A key factor in the development of a settlement under Rome rule is its pre-Roman history (if any). Whether a settlement had been a Phoenician colony, a Numidian city heavily influenced (or not) by Punic culture or a city newly founded in the Roman period, could make a huge difference in the way that a site was laid out, the deities that were worshipped in the Roman period and it might influence the types of construction that were built in a particular time frame. Given the range of factors that could affect city development, it is not a surprise that we have seen many different responses in urban architecture, inscriptions and city life after the region's incorporation into the Roman Empire. The Romans governed North Africa for centuries, during which there was considerable scope for peculiarly local devel- opments, albeit these city-specific developments took place within a general schema of 'Roman' urbanism – an urbanism that had its own set of structures and practices associated with it. Local changes were themselves the product of a range of actors who shaped their environments according to their tastes but who also took account of developments at Rome and in major cities; Carthage, Lepcis, Caesarea and other regional and provincial capitals must always have served as models and as drivers for competition. As we have seen and as we should expect, the range of actors also varied from city to city and changed over time. Imperial officials, even emperors, engaged with some urban communities and their built environment. More were left to their own devices, although governors and legionary legates must have acted as role models through their activities at cities, such as Lambaesis and, presumably, Carthage. These figures, who would have experience of the world outside Africa, could act as a conduit to wider Mediterranean concepts of the city and city-living. The desire to compete with and impress the elite of the imperial bureaucracy must have created an impeteus to construction even if the funding for the buildings was normally local.

Change & Continuity

It is obvious that although there are moments of major political and religious change that could have a considerable impact on the urban environment – such as the Roman conquest and the emergence of the Christian Empire – there were also considerable continuities in urban culture across antiquity. So while there was a gradual adoption by pre-existing Punic and Numidian urban societies of Roman building types and potentially the rituals associated with them, these changes partly took place within a pre-existing cultural framework that constrained the developments. In some ways the story of Roman Africa is the enduring nature of pre-Roman culture throughout centuries of Roman rule coupled with the ability and need of sections of the urban population to incorporate Mediterranean-wide culture and methods of expressing status.

The construction of the 'Roman' city took place over several centuries and the rate of building of individual structure types varied immensely, depending on the permeability of local cultures with regard to specific sets of cultural values associated with structures, but also because of the cost of the buildings and trends within wider society. Even in veteran colonies the construction of Roman building types was a gradual process, due to the need to finance the construction. By the fourth century, apart from the deities worshipped at a city and the way that it was laid out, there seem to be few differences in the types of structure that a city of Punic or Roman origin would construct. Instead differences seem to be the consequence of finance and connectedness with other African cities and the rest of the Mediterranean world. However, this masks the phases by which this Romano-African city was created. Taking the amphitheatre as an example, both Punic cities (e.g. Thysdrus, Utica and Lepcis) and Roman foundations (e.g. Carthage and Lambaesis) built them, primarily in the course of the second and early third centuries (Laurence et al. 2011). However, when we examine phases of construction a subtler picture emerges. The early builders of amphitheatres were strongly connected to Roman power either as residences of the governor (Carthage, Thysdrus and Utica), the capital of a client king (Caesarea) or in Theveste's case as a veteran colony and former location of the legion. The exception to this rule, Lepcis Magna, was a key ally of Rome from the first century BC onwards. From the second century the populace of a wider network of large cities with non-Roman origins such as Sabratha, Hadrumetum and Tipasa, along with cities like Lambaesis, moved to construct amphitheatres. The sole new (probably) fourth-century amphitheatre, at Sitifis, was again connected to the state. By the fourth century a variety of cities had constructed amphitheatres and the divide between those cities that had amphitheatres (and equally circuses) and those without was conditioned more by city size and wealth than their cultural origins. Slightly different patterns can be observed with the other traditional Roman build-ings types – baths, theatres, *fora*, market buildings. All, however, demonstrate a slow increase in popularity from the first to the second centuries, a dramatic expansion in the late second to early third centuries, with what appears to be an unsustainable peak in activity under Severus and Caracalla, low levels of construction in the third century, with recovery, most notably in bathing establishments, in the fourth century.

As with buildings, gradual evolution with substantial continuities of practice over time, have been observed in linguistics, religion and the naming of magistracies, par-ticularly during the first and second centuries, so that by the end of the second century the use of Punic in inscriptions had ended and the old Punic magistracies had disappeared in favour of *duumviri* and *aediles*. Religious belief and practice is a more complicated area to sum up with, on the one hand, a gradual transformation in the way that deities were named (although not necessarily conceived of) coupled with substantial temple construction in many cities, and on the other, the potentially marked caesura caused by conversion to Christianity and the rejection of the old deities. In terms of the cityscape this change led to the destruction and conversion of temples but it also created a whole new class of public building into which the community poured its energies and money. So there was a change in religious focus but sacred spaces were still built, attended and processed to and from. In the early fifth century the population could still draw on supernatural powers to protect their city, only now it was Christ and the saints rather than Baal/Saturn or Tanit/Caelestis and for a while both systems held some power over the city. This is a simplification of a complex process but it is important to note that Christianisation did not end religious building, it just changed its focus. What Christianisation did do though was create a new urban elite, in its bishops and priests, who could act as a counterweight to urban, provincial and imperial authority in a way that pagan priests had not (see Chapter 3), potentially providing a protective shield to ordinary provincials against the arbitrary acts of the powerful and the harshness of imperial law. The bishops were still a part of the elite though and alongside the churches they constructed sumptu-ous houses and private bath suites. Even the Donatist hierarchy, which was frequently in conflict with the imperial authorities during the fourth and fifth centuries, still operated as part of a Roman urban civilisation through the construction of churches and martyr shrines.

Acculturation

Assessments of 'Romanisation' or acculturation are complicated by the fact that north Africa and Rome were part of a wider Mediterranean culture despite its own local peculiarities (see Shaw 2003 for a debate on African insularity and connectedness).

Defining 'Roman' elements has been complex. Even when it is relatively easy to identify a building largely or wholly derived from Roman cultural practices – the amphitheatre or bath house for example – there is a debate to be had about what the construction of 'Roman' buildings means for culture and identity within the cities of Africa. Cherry argues that the construction of buildings does not demonstrate that the population were really becoming more Roman, that the adoption of Roman-type structures such as bath houses are just a sensible adoption of a useful building type that says little about cultural identity or the adoption of a set of values (Cherry 1998: 82–3). This can be challenged, however. The construction of a set of baths was not just about the provision of hot rooms for sweating, a *palaestra* for exercise and the cold pools but about a particular way of behaving, of interacting with other bathers. Bathing in purpose-built structures was a very different experience than washing with water drawn from a cistern, well or river (Laurence et al. 2011). Additionally, North African peoples outside of Rome's cultural orbit do not seem to have built baths or amphitheatres. So whilst we might argue that the Garamantes would have found it hard to have a bathing culture as opulent and wasteful as that maintained at Lepcis to their north, they could have adopted theatres or amphitheatres but they made a positive choice not to do so (it seems unlikely that no Garamantian trader ever came into contact with Roman building types in Oea, Sabratha or Lepcis). On the other hand, Juba II and his circle made a positive choice to echo Roman and wider Hellenistic models of building at Caesarea. Incorporation into Rome's sphere of influence mattered then as to whether a people adopted Roman-style buildings, but it was not a given that populations who had knowledge of Roman buildings would construct their own variants. It was a proactive decision on the part of at least some within a community to construct these structures, to incorporate themselves and everyone who used the baths or attended the amphitheatre, or even passed through the city with its inscriptions (in their scope and content distinctively 'Roman' in Africa) and statues, into a wider Roman style of life (contra Cherry 1998: 84). Even if there was not a conscious desire to become Roman through the construction of these buildings, the provision of these facilities would have resulted in acculturation between locals and the wider culture and the incorporation of Roman concepts of proper behaviour.

There was a gradual transformation at many cities but there was clearly no need for communities to adopt all elements of 'Roman' urbanism. The most obvious example of this is in orthogonal city planning. Although some cities with pre-Roman roots, such as Lepcis, Sabratha and Tipasa, had street-grid systems from the first century BC onwards and Roman foundations such as Carthage, Ammaedara, Sufetula or Thamugadi were built with them, many African populations clearly believed they were unnecessary. Native settlements such as Thuburbo Maius and Thugga never had them and over time those of Thamugadi and Cuicul were ignored and undermined, in the case of the former by the corporate body of the city itself by building the *capitolium* at an angle to the rest of the city. Clearly as colonies these cities were no less 'Roman' than Lepcis but the populations had other priorities and needs that did not chime with the maintenance of a street grid; the Romano-African concept of the city was fluid enough to incorporate those that were rigorously planned and those that developed organically. Similarly the slow growth in Roman-style construction in the first century AD should not be seen as local populations consciously resisting a 'global' Roman culture through the preservation of past tradition and the refusal to adopt Roman styles of architecture or nomenclature for their gods, but as a sign of a lack of penetration of Roman concepts of civic space and urban rituals into Africa. The speed with which Roman-style buildings and urban space was constructed in the second century AD across Roman Africa demonstrates that when city populations and elites became aware of the possibilities for increasing personal and civic status through urban construction they quickly bought into and adapted a new cultural set of structures whilst often preserving elements of their ancestral culture. So the people of Thugga may have constructed a temple to Saturn to replace an area sacred to Baal in the early second century but it was on the same emplacement (see Chapter 3). The site therefore demonstrates continuity of sacred space coupled with changes in nomenclature and monumentalisation. The way the population viewed the god might have been changed by this monumentalisation but only within a wider frame-work of continuity. Over time then urban populations' expectations about what their city should look like would have changed. The fourth-century AD citizen of Thugga would have had a very different conception of the city and probably their own iden-tity than a similar citizen in the first century BC. The city would, of course, have looked different but it would also have functioned differently. Not only had the legal divisions between Roman and conquered been erased but over many generations the expectations of the cityscape would have changed as the functioning of the city and the inhabitants' perceptions of what buildings were essential for urban life evolved.

Africa Romana

The urban culture of Roman Africa was then varied, with different local condi-tions creating a specific local form of that urbanism, even if it was within a wider Romano-African framework. A Calaman visiting Carthage would have recognised the form of urbanism on display even if it was being reproduced on a scale that their home town could not match. The bath house, monumental temples (then churches), the forum, triumphal arches, theatre, statues, inscriptions were all replicated across the region, albeit to suit different specific concerns in different places. The specific 'localness' of the urban form within this wider framework is the key feature of this culture. Local needs (or desires) dictated when a specific building was constructed. Not building an amphitheatre or theatre was not a rejection of Rome but might be an example of financial probity or the consequence of investment in bathing (for example). Likewise, taking any hint of the adoption of Roman culture as indicating wholesale Romanising and any maintenance of pre-Roman customs as a rejection of Roman culture would be foolish. In reality, as it has been recognised in the last decade or so, it was entirely possible for individuals and communities to have multiple identities. So an inhabitant of Lepcis Magna, such as Annobal Tapapius Rufus, son of Himilcho, who paid for the theatre, erecting bilingual Latin/Punic inscriptions could have regarded himself as a loyal member of the Empire, a member of Lepcis' elite and part of a wider Phoenician/ Punic culture (Plate 3). Likewise, a fourth-century Donatist bishop could have viewed themselves as a loyal member of the Empire, a member of their own city's elite, a member of a widespread but varying Romano-African culture, but also as a leader of a sect that was often opposed to imperial policy.

This book has demonstrated that the African cities were not identical copies of each other or Rome but, more importantly, that they were never meant to be. Local elites and communities constructed environments that reflected their own views about what a city should look like, informed by both their own experiences of other cities and their own expectations, which had been inculcated by their culture and environment. Once a bath or an amphitheatre had been constructed the rituals and performances that took place in them would have helped to inform the citizens about proper urban behaviour. Over time, as more and more buildings were constructed, the urban citizen and the city would have been increasingly affected by elements of a 'Roman' or Mediterranean-wide culture, albeit a culture that was mediated by their Punic, Numidian or veteran past. The remains of Lepcis or Carthage as they appear to us are then a product of several centuries of populations adopting elements of Roman culture and merging that with aspects of pre-existing cultures.

Bibliography

Journal Abbreviations:
AntAfr – Antiquités Africaines
AJPh – American Journal of Philology
ANRW – Aufstieg und Niedergang der römischen Welt
BAR Int.Ser. – British Archaeological Reports, International Series.
BCTH – Bulletin archéologique du Comité des Travaux Historiques et Scientifiques
CRAI – Comptes rendus de l'Académie des Inscriptions et Belles-Lettres
JECS – Journal of Early Christian Studies
JRA – Journal of Roman Archaeology
JRS – Journal of Roman Studies
LS – Libyan Studies
MEFRA – Mélanges de l'École Française de Rome: antiquité
RA – Revue Africaine

Adams, J.N. 1994. 'Latin and Punic in contact? The case of the Bu Njem ostraca', *JRS* 84: 87–112.
——— 1999. 'The poets of Bu Njem', *JRS* 89: 109–34.
——— 2004. *Bilingualism and the Latin Language*, Cambridge.
Alexander, M.A. & Ennaifer, M. 1973. *Corpus des mosaïques de Tunisie. 1.1. Utique, insulae I, II et III*, Tunis.
Alexander, M.A., Ben Abed-Ben Khader, A., Besrour, S., Mansour, B. & Soren, D. 1980. *Corpus des mosaïques de Tunisie. 2.1. Thuburbo Majus, Les mosaïques de la région du forum*, Tunis.
Allais, Y. 1939. 'La 'Maison d'Europe' à Djemila', *RA* 83: 35–44.
——— 1953. 'Djemila: Le quartier a l'est du forum des Sévères', *RA* 97: 48–65.
Aounallah, S. 2001. *Le Cap Bon, jardin de Carthage: recherches d'épigraphie et d'histoire romano-africaines, 146 a.C-235 p.C*, Bordeaux.
Aubet, M.E. 1995. 'From trading post to town in the Phoenician-Punic World', Cunliffe, B. & Keay, S. (eds) *Social Complexity and the Development of Towns in Iberia: from the Copper Age to the Second Century AD*, Proceedings of the British Academy 86: 47–65.
Ballu, A. 1897. *Les ruines de Timgad; Antique Thamugadi*, Paris.

———— 1903. *Les ruines de Timgad; Antique Thamugadi. Nouvelle découvertes*, Paris.

———— 1911. *Les ruines de Timgad; Sept années de découvertes*, Paris.

Barton, I.M. 1972. *Africa in the Roman Empire*, Accra.

———— 1982. 'Capitoline temples in Italy and the provinces (especially Africa)', *ANRW* II.12.1, Berlin: 259–342.

Bayliss, R. 2004. *Provincial Cilicia and the archaeology of Temple Conversion*, BAR Int.Ser. 1281, Oxford.

Bénabou, M. 1976. *La Resistance Africaine à la Romanisation*, Paris.

———— 'Les romains ont-ils conquis l'Afrique', *Annales: Économies Sociétés Civilisations* 33: 83–8.

Bénichou-Safar, H. 2004. *Le Tophet de Salammbô à Carthage: essai de Reconstitution*, Collection de l'École Française de Rome 342, Rome.

Ben Younes, H. 1995. 'Tunisie', Krings, V. (ed.) *La civilisation phénicienne et punique: Manuel de recherche*, Leiden: 796–827.

———— 2007. 'Interculturality and the Punic Funerary World', *Mortuary Landscapes of North Africa*, Phoenix Supplementary Vol. 43, Toronto: 32–42.

Berthier, A. 1980. 'Un habitat punique a Constantine', *AntAfr* 16: 13–26.

Berthier, A. & Charlier, R. 1955. *Le sanctuaire punique d'El-Hofra à Constantine,* Paris.

Berthier, A. & Leglay, M. 1958. 'Le sanctuaire du sommet et les stèles à Ba'al-Saturne de Tiddis', *Libyca* 6.1: 23–74.

Birebent, J. 1962. *Aquae Romanae*, Algiers.

Birley, A.R. 1988. *The African emperor: Septimius Severus*, London.

Boeswillwald, E., Cagnat, R. & Ballu, A. 1892–1904. *Timgad: une cité africaine sous l'empire romain*, Paris. Vols 1–8.

Bomgardner, D.L. 2000. *The story of the Roman Amphitheatre*, New York.

Bowden, W. 2001. 'Church builders and church building late-antique Epirus', Lavan, L. (ed.) *Recent research in Late-Antique Urbanism*, JRA Supplementary Series 42; Portsmouth: 57–68.

Brett, M. & Fentress, E. 1996. *The Berbers*, Oxford.

Broughton, T.R.S. 1929. *The Romanization of Africa Proconsularis*, Baltimore.

Brouquier-Reddé, V. 1992. *Temples et cultes de Tripolitaine*, Paris.

Brown, P. 1971. *The World of Late Antiquity*, London.

Cadotte, A. 2007. *La Romanisation des dieux: L'interpretatio romana en Afrique du Nord sous le Haut-Empire*, Religions in the Graeco-Roman World 158, Leiden.

Cagnat, R. 1909. *Carthage, Timgad, Tébessa et les villes antiques de l'Afrique du Nord*, Paris.

———— 1912. *L'armée romaine d'afrique*, Paris.

Camps, G. 1954. 'L'inscription de Béja et le problème des Dii Mauri', *RA* 98: 233–60.

Casson, L. 2001. *Libraries in the Ancient World*, New Haven.

Chatelain, M.L. 1918. *Les Recherches Archéologiques au Maroc 'Volubilis' Conférence faite au centre de perfectionnement de Meknès.*

Chelbi, F., Paskoff, R. & Trousset, P. 1995. 'La baie d'Utique et son évolution depuis l'Antiquité: une réévaluation géoarchéologique', *AntAfr*. 31: 7–52.

Cherry, D. 1998. *Frontier and Society in Roman North Africa*, Oxford.

Cintas, P. 1947. 'La Sanctuaire Punique de Sousse', *RA* 91: 1–80.

Condron, F. 1998. 'Ritual, space and politics; reflections in the archaeological record of social developments in Lepcis Magna, Tripolitania', *TRAC. 97. Proceedings of the Seventh Annual Theoretical Roman Archaeological Conference*, Oxford: 42–52.

Constans, L. 1916. *Gigthis, étude d'histoire et d'archéologie sur un emporium de la petite Syrte*, Paris.

Cooley, A. 2007. 'Septimius Severus: the Augustan emperor', Swain, S., Harrison, S. & Elsner, J. (eds) *Severan Culture*, Cambridge: 290–326.

Crawford, M. (ed.) 1996. *Roman Statutes*, London.

Daniels, C.M. 1989. 'Excavation and fieldwork amongst the Garamantes', *LS* 20: 45–61.

De Ruyt, C. 1983. *Macellum*, Louvain-Le-Neuve.

Desanges, J. 1978. *Recherches sur l'activité des Méditerranéens aux confines de l'Afrique (VIe siècle avant J.-C. – IVe siècle après J.-C.)*, Collection de l'École Française de Rome 38, Rome.

Di Vita, A. 1982. 'Gli emporia di Tripolitania dall'età di Massinissa a Diocleziano: un profile storico–istituzionale', *ANRW* II.10.2, Berlin: 515–95.

———— 1990. 'Sismi, urbanistica e cronologia assoluta', *L'Afrique dans l'occident Romain*, Collection de l'École Française de Rome 134, Rome: 425–94.

Dore, J. 1988. 'Pottery and the history of Roman Tripolitania: evidence from Sabratha and the UNESCO Libyan Valleys Survey', *LS* 19: 61–85.

Duliere, C. 1974. *Corpus des mosaïques de Tunisie. 1.2 Utique: Les mosaïques in situ en dehors des insulae I, II et III*, Tunis.

Duliere, C., Slim, H., Alexander, M.A., Ostrow, S., Pedley, J.G. & Soren, D. 1996. *Corpus des mosaïques de Tunisie. 3.1 Thysdrus, El Jem: Quartier Sud-Ouest*, Tunis.

Dunbabin, K.M.D. 1978. *The Mosaics of Roman North Africa: Studies in Iconography and Patronage*, Oxford.

Duncan-Jones, R.P. 1963. 'City population in Roman Africa', *JRS* 53: 85–90.

———— 1974. *The economy of the Roman Empire: quantitative studies*, London.

———— 2004. 'Economic change and the transition to late antiquity', Swain, S. & Edwards, M. *Approaching Late Antiquity*, Oxford.

Duval, N. 1982a. 'L'Urbanisme de Sufetula', *ANRW* II.10.2, Berlin: 596–632.

———— 1982b. 'Topographie et urbanisme d'Ammaedara', *ANRW* II.10.2, Berlin: 633–671.

Duval, P-M. 1946. *Cherchel et Tipasa*, Paris.

Dyggve, E. 1951. *History of Salonitan Christianity*, Oslo.

Eadie, J.W. & Humphrey, J.H. 1977. 'The topography of the southeast quarter of later Roman Carthage', Humphrey, J.H. (ed.) *Excavations at Carthage 1976 conducted by the University of Michigan*, Vol. 3, Ann Arbor: 1–19.

Fantar, M.H. 1987. *Kerkouane: une Cité Punique au Cap-Bon*, Tunis.

Fentress, E. 1979. *Numidia and the Roman Army. BAR. Int.Ser.* 53. Oxford.

———— 1984. 'Frontier culture and politics at Timgad', *BCTH*, n.s. 17B: 399–407.

———— 1989. 'Sétif, les thermes du Ve siècle', *L'Africa Romana* 6: 3211–337.

———— 1990. 'The economy of an inland city: Sétif', *L'afrique dans l'occident Romain*, Collection de l'École Française de Rome 134, Rome: 117–28.

Février, P-A. 1964. 'Notes sur le développement urbain en Afrique du Nord, les exemples compares de Djemila et de Sétif', *Cahiers Archéologiques* 14: 1–47.

———— 1967. 'Aux origines de l'occupation romaine dans les hautes plaines de Sétif', *Les Cahiers de Tunisie* 15: 51–64.

———— (1968) *Djemila*, Alger.

———— 1978. 'Le culte des morts dans les communautés chrétiennes durant le IIIe siècle', *Atti del IX congresso internazionale di archeologia cristiana, Roma, 1975*, Vatican City, 1.211–74.

———— 1982a. 'Urbanisation et Urbanisme de l'Afrique Romaine', *ANRW* II.10.2, Berlin: 321–97.

———— 1982b. 'Le fait urbain dans le Maghreb du IIIème siècle. Les signes d'une crise?', *La Méditerranée de Paul-Albert Février, Vol II*, Rome; Aix-en-Provence, 813–39.

Fishwick, D. 1987. *The Imperial Cult in the Latin West. Vol. 1.2*, Leiden.

———— 2002. *The Imperial Cult in the Latin West. Vol. 3: Provincial Cult; Part 2: The Provincial Priesthood*, Leiden.

Fontana, S. 2001. 'Leptis Magna. The Romanization of a major African city through burial evidence', Keay, S. & Terrenato, N. (eds) *Italy and the West: Comparative Issues in Romanization*, Oxford: 161–72.

Foucher, L. 1961. *Découvertes à Thysdrus en 1960*, Tunis.

———— 1964. *Hadrumetum*, Paris.

Frend, W.H.C. 1952. *The Donatist Church: A Movement of Protest in Roman North Africa*, Oxford.

Gager, J.G. 1992. *Curse tablets and binding spells from the ancient world*, New York.

Gauckler, M.P. 1899. 'Découvertes à Carthage', *CRAI* 156–65.

Gerner Hansen, C. 2002. 'Carthage: results of the Swedish excavations 1979–1983, Vol. 1, A Roman bath in Carthage', *Skrifter utgivna av Svenska Institutet I Rom*. 4; 54: 1.

Gibbon, E. 1776–88. 1998. *The Decline and Fall of the Roman Empire*, Ware.

Giddens, A. 1984. *The Constitution of Society; Outline of the Theory of Structuration*, Cambridge.

Girard, S. 1984. 'Banasa préromaine un état de la question', *AntAfr* 20: 11–93.

Golvin, J-C. & Leveau, P. 1979. 'L'amphithéâtre et le théâtre-amphithéâtre de Cherchel: Monuments à spectacles et histoire urbaine à Caesarea de Maurétanie', *MEFRA* 91.2: 817–43.

Goodchild, R.G. 1965. 'The unfinished 'Imperial' Baths of Lepcis Magna', *Libya Antiqua* 2: 15–27.

Goodchild, R.G., Reynolds J.M. & Herington C.J. 1958. 'The Temple of Zeus at Cyrene', *Papers of the British School at Rome* 26: 30–62.

Goodchild, R.G. & Ward-Perkins, J.B. 1953. 'The Christian Antiquities of Tripolitania', *Archaeologica* 95: 1–84.

Gros, P. & Deneauve, J. 1980. 'Hypothèses sur le centre monumental de la Carthage Romaine, d'après les recherché récentes sur la colline de Byrsa', *CRAI*: 299–332.

Groupe de Recherches sur l'Afrique antique, ed. 1993. *Les Flavii de Cillium. Étude architecturale, épigraphique, historique et littéraire du mausolée de Kasserine (CIL, VIII, 211-216)*, Collection de l'École française de Rome, 169, Rome.

Gsell, S. 1901. *Les monuments antiques de l'Algérie*, Paris.

Gui, I. Duval, N. & Caillet, J-P. 1992. *Basiliques chrétiennes d'afrique du nord: I Inventaire de l'algérie, texte*, Paris.

Haynes, D.E.L. 1955. *The Antiquities of Tripolitania*, Tripoli.

Howard Carter, T. 1965. 'Western Phoenicians at Lepcis Magna', *American Journal of Archaeology*, 69.2: 123–32.

Humphrey, J.H. 1986. *Roman Circuses: Arenas for Chariot Racing*, London.

Humphrey, J.H. Sear, F. & Vickers, M. 1972–73. 'Aspects of the circus at Lepcis Magna', *Libya Antiqua* 9–10: 25–97.

Hurst, H.R. 1994. *Excavations at Carthage: The British Mission, Vol. II.1, The Circular Harbour, North Side*. Oxford.

Isserlin, B.S.J. 1974. *Motya, a Phoenician and Carthaginian city in Sicily: a report of the excavations undertaken during the years 1961–65. Vol. 1*, Leiden.

Janon, M. 2005. *Lambèse*, Ollioules.

Jodin, A. 1966. *Mogador: Comptoir Phénicien du Maroc Atlantique*, Rabat.

——— 1987. *Volvbilis Regia Ivbae*, Paris.

Johnson, M.J. 1997. 'Pagan-Christian burial practices of the fourth century: shared tombs?' *JECS* 5.1: 37–59.

Jordan, D.R. 1988. 'New *defixiones* from Carthage', Humphrey, J. (ed.) *The Circus and Byzantine Cemetery at Carthage*, Ann Arbor.

Jouffroy, H. 1986. *La Construction Publique en Italie et dans L'Afrique Romaine*, Strasbourg.

Kenrick, P.M. 1986. *Excavations at Sabratha (1948–51)*, London.

Khanoussi, M. 1992. 'Thugga sous le Haut-Empire: une ville double?' *L'Africa Romana* 10.1: 597–602.

——— Ritter, S. & von Rummel, P. 2004–05. 'The German-Tunisian Project at Dougga: First Results of the Excavations South of the Maison du Trifolium', *AntAfr* 40–1: 43–66.

Lancel, S. (ed.) 1982. *Byrsa: mission archéologique francaise a Carthage. Vol. 2, Rapports préliminaires sur les fouilles 1977–1978*, Collection de l'École Francaise de Rome 41/2, Rome.

————— 1995a. 'Vie des cites et urbanisme partim occident', Krings, V. (ed.) *La civilisation phé-nicienne et punique: Manuel de recherche*, Leiden: 370–88.

————— 1995b. *Carthage*, Oxford.

Lancel, S. & Morel, J-P. 1992. 'La colline de Byrsa: les vestiges Puniques', Ennabli, A. (ed.) *Pour Sauver Carthage. Exploration et conservation de la cité punique, romaine et byzantine*, Paris: 43–68.

Laroui, A. 1977. *The History of the Maghrib, an Interpretive Essay*, Princeton.

Lassus, J. 1981. *La Forteresse Byzantine de Thamugadi: Fouilles à Timgad 1938–1956 1*. Paris.

Laurence, R., Esmonde Cleary, S. & Sears, G. Forthcoming 2011. *The Cities of the Roman West*, Cambridge.

Le Bohec, Y. 1989. *La troisième légion auguste*, Paris.

————— 2005. *Histoire de l'afrique romaine*, Paris.

Le Glay, M. 1961–66. *Saturne Africain: Monuments I and II*, Paris.

————— 1966. *Saturne Africain, Histoire*, Paris.

Leone, A. 2007. 'Changing urban landscapes: burials in North African cities from the Late Antique to Byzantine periods', Stone, D.L. & Stirling, L.M. (eds) *Mortuary Landscapes of North Africa*, Phoenix Supplementary Vol. 43, Toronto: 164–203.

Lepelley, C. 1981. *Les cites de l'afrique romaine au bas-empire, II*, Paris.

————— 1994. 'La musée des statues divines. La volonté de sauvegarder le patrimoine artis-tique païen à L'époque théodosienne', *Cahiers Archéologiques 42: 5–15*, Paris.

Lequément, R. 1967. 'Fouilles a l'amphithéâtre de Tébessa (1965–66)', *Bulletin d'Archéologie Algérienne 2*: 107–22.

Leschi, L. 1947. 'Découvertes récentes a Timgad: Aqua Septimiana Felix', *CRAI*: 87–99.

————— 1959. *Études d'épigraphie, d'archéologie et d'historie africaines*, Paris.

Leveau, P. 1984. *Caesarea de Maurétanie: une ville romaine et ses campagnes*, Collection de l'École Française de Rome 70, Rome.

Leynaud, Msgr. 1922. *Les catacombes africaines*, Algiers.

Lézine, A. 1968. *Carthage-Utique*, Paris.

Longerstay, M. 1995. 'Libye', Krings, V. (ed.) *La civilisation phénicienne et punique: Manuel de recherche*, Leiden: 828–44.

Lynch, K. 1960. *The Image of the City*, Cambridge.

MacDonald, W.L. 1986. *The Architecture of the Roman Empire: 2 An Urban Appraisal*, New Haven.

MacMullen, R. 1963. *Soldier and Civilian in the Late Roman Empire*, Cambridge.

————— 1966. 'Provincial Languages in the Roman Empire', *AJPh* 87: 1–17.

————— 1982. 'The epigraphic habit in the Roman Empire', *AJPh* 103: 233–46.

————— 1988. *Corruption and the Decline of Rome*, New Haven.

Marcillet-Jaubert, J. 1970. 'Deux dédicaces à Neptune trouvées à Lambèse', *BCTH* n.s. 5: 213–20.

Marichal, R. 1992. *Les ostraca de Bu Njem*, Tripoli.

Matthews, J.F. 1976. 'Mauretania in Ammianus and the Notitia', Mann, J.C., Goodburn, R. & Bartholomew, P. (eds) *Aspects of the 'Notitia Dignitatum': Papers Presented to the Conference in Oxford, December 13 to 15, 1974*, Oxford, BAR 15: 157–88.

Mattingly, D.J. 1988a. 'Oil for export? A comparison of Libyan, Spanish and Tunisian olive oil production in the Roman empire', *JRA* 1: 33–56.

————— 1988b. 'The olive boom. Oil surpluses, wealth and power in Roman Tripolitania', *LS* 19: 21–41.

————— 1995. *Roman Tripolitania*, London.

————— 1996. 'From one colonialism to another: imperialism and the Maghreb', Webster, J. & Cooper, N. (eds) *Roman Imperialism: Post-Colonial Perspectives*, Leicester Archaeology Monographs No 3. Leicester: 49–69.

———— 2007. 'The African way of death: burial rituals beyond the Roman Empire', Stone, D.L. & Stirling, L.M. (eds) *Mortuary Landscapes of North Africa*, Phoenix Supplementary Vol. 43, Toronto: 138–63.

Maurin, L. 1995. '*Pagus Mercurialis Veteranorum Medelitanorum*. Implantations veterans dans la vallée de l'oued Miliane. Le dossier épigraphique', *MEFRA* 107.1: 97–135.

Merlin, A. 1908. *Le Temple d'Apollon à Bulla Regia*, Paris.

Millar, F. 1968. 'Local cultures in the Roman Empire', *JRS* 58: 126-153.

Mohamedi, A., Benmansour, A., Amamra, A.A. & Fentress, E. 1991. *Fouilles de Sétif (1977-1984), 5eme Supplement au Bulletin d'Archéologie Algérienne*, Algiers.

Moore, J.P. 2007. 'The "Mausoleum Culture" of Africa Proconsularis', Stone, D.L. & Stirling, L.M. (eds) *Mortuary Landscapes of North Africa*, Phoenix Supplementary Vol. 43, Toronto: 75–109.

Moralee, J. 2006. 'The Stones of St. Theodore: Disfiguring the Pagan Past in Christian Gerasa', *JECS* 14.2: 183–215.

Morestin, H. 1980. *Le Temple B de Volubilis*, Paris.

Neuru, L. 1992. 'Le secteur nord-est de la ville', Ennabli, A. (ed.) *Pour Sauver Carthage: exploration et conservation de la cité punique, romaine et Byzantine*, Paris: 135–42.

Nielsen, I. 1990. *Thermae et balnea*, Aarhus.

Niemeyer, H.G. 1992. 'Chronologie et caractères de l'habitat primitif: premiers résultats: 1986–1988', Ennabli, A. (ed.) *Pour Sauver Carthage. Exploration et conservation de la cité punique, romaine et byzantine*, Paris: 38–41.

———— 1995. 'Expansion et colonisation', Krings, V. (ed.) *La civilisation phénicienne et punique: Manuel de recherche*, Leiden: 247–67.

Peña, J.T. 1998. 'The mobilization of state olive oil in Roman Africa: the evidence of late 4th-c. ostraca from Carthage', *Carthage Papers. The early colony's economy, water supply, a public bath and the mobilization of state olive oil*, JRA Supplementary Series 28, Portsmouth, RI: 117–238.

Picard, G.C. 1954. *Les religions de l'afrique antique*, Paris.

———— 1964. 'Un palais du IVe siècle a Carthage', *CRAI*: 101–18.

———— 1976. La date du théâtre de Cherchel et les débuts de l'architecture théâtrale dans les provinces romaines d'Occident, *CRAI*: 386–97.

———— 1984. Le temple du musée à Mactar, *Revue Archéologique*: 13–28.

Poinssot, C. 1958. *Les Ruines de Dougga*, Tunis.

Ponsich, M. 1982. 'Lixus: informations archéologiques', *ANRW* II.10.2, Berlin: 817–49.

Potter, T.W. 1995. *Towns in Late Antiquity: Iol Caesarea and its context*, Sheffield.

Quinn, J.C. 2009. 'North Africa', Erskine, A. (ed.) *A Companion to Ancient History*, Malden: 260–72.

Rakob, F. 1992. 'L'Habitat Ancien et le système urbanistique', Ennabli, A. (ed.) *Pour Sauver Carthage. Exploration et conservation de la cité punique, romaine et byzantine*, Paris: 29–37.

Rebuffat, R. 1989. 'Notes sur le camp Romain de Gholaia', *LS* 20: 155–67.

Reynolds, J.M. & Ward-Perkins, J.B. 2009. *Inscriptions of Roman Tripolitania*, Rome. Enhanced electronic reissue, G. Bodard & C. Roueché – http://irt.kcl.ac.uk/irt2009/.

Rives, J. 1994. 'Venus Genetrix outside Rome', *Phoenix*, 48.4: 294–306.

———— 1995. *Religion and authority in Roman Carthage from Augustus to Constantine*, Oxford.

Roller, D.W. 2003. *The World of Juba II and Kleopatra Selene*, New York.

Saint-Amans S. 2004. *Topographie religieuse de Thugga (Dougga): Ville romaine d'Afrique proconsulaire (Tunisie)*, Paris.

Sear, F. 2006. *Roman Theatres: An Architectural Study*, Oxford.

Sears, G.M. 2007. *Late Roman African Urbanism: Continuity and Transformation in the City*, BAR Int.Ser. 1693, Oxford.

Shaw, B.D. 1983. 'Soldiers and society: the army in Numidia', *Opus* 2: 133–59.

———— 2003. 'A peculiar island: Maghrib and Mediterranean', *Mediterranean Historical Review* 18.2: 93–125.

———— 2007. *Cult and Belief in Punic and Roman Africa*, version 1.2, Princeton/Stanford Working Papers in Classics – www.princeton.edu/~pswpc/pdfs/shaw/090705.pdf.

Slim, H. 1976. 'Thysdrus', Stillwell, R., MacDonald, W.L. & McAllister, M.H. (eds) *The Princeton Encyclopedia of Classical Sites*, Princeton: 919–20.

Stewart, P. 2003. *Statues in Roman Society: Representation and Response*, Oxford.

Stevens, S.T. 1996. 'Transitional neighbourhoods and suburban frontiers in Late- and post-Roman Carthage', Mathisen, R.W. & Sivan, H.S. (eds) *Shifting Frontiers in Late Antiquity*, Aldershot: 187–200.

Stone, D.L. 2007. 'Monuments on the Margins: Interpreting the First Millennium B.C.E. Rock-cut tombs (Haouanet) of North Africa', *Mortuary Landscapes of North Africa*, Phoenix Supplementary Vol. 43, Toronto: 43–74.

Teichner, F. 1996. 'Signa Venerandae Christianae Religionis: On the conversion of pagan sanctuaries in the dioceses of Africa and Aegyptus', *LS* 27: 53–66.

Thébert, Y. 1978. 'Romanisation et déromanisation en afrique: histoire décolonisée ou histoire inversée?', *Annales: Économies Sociétés Civilisations* 33: 64–82.

———— 2003. *Thermes romains d'Afrique du Nord et leur contexte méditerranéen: études d'histoire et d'archéologie*, Rome.

Thomas, E.V. 2007. *Monumentality and the Roman Empire: Architecture in the Antonine age*, Oxford.

Trifilò, F. 2008. 'Power, architecture and community in the distribution of honorary statues in Roman public space', Fenwick, C., Wiggins, M. & Wythe, D. (eds) *Proceedings of the Seventeenth Annual Theoretical Roman Archaeology Conference, London 2007*, Oxford: 109–20.

Van der Veen, M. 1992. 'Garamantian Agriculture', *LS* 23: 7–40.

Ward-Perkins, J.B. & Kenrick, P. (eds) 1993. *The Severan Buildings of Lepcis Magna; an architectural survey*, London.

Ward-Perkins, B. 2005. *The Fall of Rome and the End of Civilisation*, Oxford.

Wells, C.M. 1992. 'Le mur de Théodose et le secteur nord-est de la ville romaine', Ennabli, A. (ed.) *Pour Sauver Carthage: exploration et conservation de la cité punique, romaine et byzantine*, Paris: 115–23.

Whitaker, J.I.S. 1921. *Motya: a Phoenician colony in Sicily*, London.

Whittaker, C.R. 1978a. 'Carthaginian imperialism in the fifth and fourth centuries', Garnsey, P. & Whittaker, C.R. (eds) *Imperialism in the Ancient World*, Cambridge: 59–90.

———— 1978b. 'Bénabou, M.: "La résistance africaine à la romanisation"', *JRS* 68: 190–2.

———— 1997. *Frontiers of the Roman Empire*, Baltimore.

White, D. 1984. *The Extramural Sanctuary of Demeter and Persephone at Cyrene, Libya. Final Reports, Vol. 1: Background and Introduction to the Excavations*, Philadelphia.

White, L.M. 1997. *The Social Origins of Christian Architecture, Volume II, Texts and Monuments for the Christian Domus Ecclesiae in its Environment*, Harvard Theological Studies 42, Baltimore.

Wild, R.A. 1984. 'The known Isis-Sarapis sanctuaries from the Roman Period', *ANRW* II.17.4, Berlin: 1739–851.

———— 1998. 'Water supply in ancient Carthage', *Carthage Papers. The early colony's economy, water supply, a public bath and the mobilization of state olive oil*, JRA Supplementary Series 28, Portsmouth: 65–102.

———— 2007. 'Urban development in the Severan Empire', Swain, S., Harrison, S. & Elsner, J. (eds) *Severan Culture*, Cambridge: 290–326.

Zimmer, G. 1989. *Locus datus decreto decurionum. Zur statuenafstellung zweier Forumsanlagen im römischen Afrika*, München.

Index

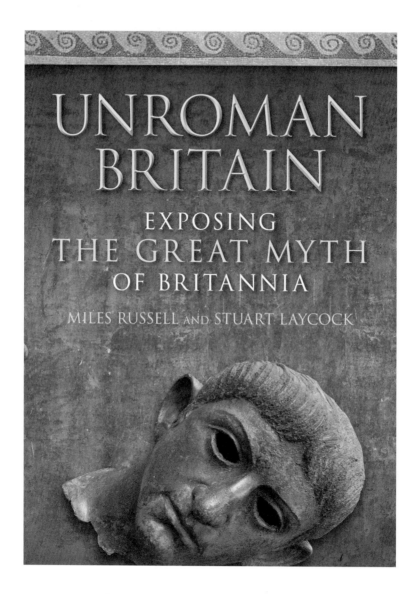

UNROMAN
BRITAIN

EXPOSING
THE GREAT MYTH
OF BRITANNIA

MILES RUSSELL AND STUART LAYCOCK

UnRoman Britain – Exposing the Great Myth of Britannia
by Miles Russell & Stuart Laycock

'[a] thrillingly provocative read' – Tom Holland, *The Sunday Times*

978 0 7524 5566 2